Cheryl Lassiter is an author whose works include:
Marked: The Witchcraft Persecution of Goodwife Unise Cole, 1656-1680
A Meet and Suitable Person: Tavernkeeping in Old Hampton,
New Hampshire, 1638-1783
A Page Out of History: A Hampton Woman in the Needletrades, 1859-1869
Her *History Matters* column can be read in the Hampton Union, The
Beachcomber, seacoastonline.com, and at lassitergang.com.

Karen Raynes is the author of a memoir of her family's store,
Marelli's Market: The First 100 Years in Hampton, New Hampshire, 1914-2014

The
QUEENS
of
HAMPTON BEACH
NEW HAMPSHIRE

The History of the Carnival Queens &
Miss Hampton Beach Beauty Pageant

1915-2015

Cheryl Lassiter & Karen Raynes

Blue Petal Press | Hampton, New Hampshire

Blue Petal Press | Hampton NH 03842

© 2016 Cheryl Lassiter and Karen Raynes

Designed by LassiterGang Media | Hampton NH

Printed in the good old USA

ISBN-13: 978-1539841180

ISBN-10: 1539841189

Front cover image: Junior Miss Hampton Beach parade float, c. 1950. Courtesy of the Hampton Historical Society.

*To all the Hampton Beach queens,
past and present.
Let not their contributions
to grace, beauty, and the enjoyment
of the beach be forgotten.*

Beauty contests seem to evoke strong opinions, both for and against. To supporters they are a form of entertainment; enjoyable social activities that help build contestants' self-confidence and poise. To detractors they are an affront to what it means to be a woman in the twenty-first century. No doubt truth can be found on both sides of the issue, but as historians we are neither for nor against beauty contests, and we happily leave it to others to argue their merits. Our mission is to tell the untold story of one of the longest-running traditions at Hampton Beach, New Hampshire—that of young women vying for the title of Queen of the beach.

That the tradition had recently passed its century mark lent timeliness and relevance to our mission, and in August 2016 we were pleased to present to the Hampton community the documentary video *100 Years At The Beach: The History of the Carnival Queens and Miss Hampton Beach Pageant, 1915-2015*. Now we are equally as pleased to present this book to the general public.

ACKNOWLEDGMENTS

Thanks to individual contributors Stephanie Lussier, Marilyn Atkinson Tilbury, Ed Parent, Tami Mallett, Carole Wheeler Walles, John Kane, Katie Widen Reardon, Betty Moore, Elly Becotte, Julene Britt, Sheila Scott, Frances Houlihan, Claire Henneka Service, Bob Dennett, Al Casassa, Fred Rice, Linda Gebhart, Louise McDevitt, Shanna Clarke, and Don McNeill. Thanks also to the Hampton Historical Society for their support.

CONTENTS

THE CARNIVAL QUEENS
1915-1940

The Carnival Queens 1915-1940

Carnival Week was created in 1915 by the Board of Trade, a business organization formed to promote Hampton Beach. Held over the Labor Day holiday, it was a way to extend the summer tourist season. The Carnival lasted until 1953 and was replaced with an August Festival the following year.

The Carnival was seven days of stage shows, featuring beautiful female performers and thrilling acts like the stunt riders Daredevil Van Norman, Allo Diavolo, and the daring gymnast Samoyoa the Great.

Along with the professional entertainers, there were civic parades and decorated automobile contests with engraved loving cups for the winning cars. There were children's day parades and historical pageants performed by

Hampton Beach Board of Trade, c. 1915. Back row l-r: Frank Callahan, Joseph S. Dudley, James Tucker. Front row l-r: J. Frank James and J.A. McAdams.

local residents. Visiting dignitaries and politicians were always on hand to give a speech or two. There were games and nightly fireworks, confetti battles, a "parade of bathing girls" who competed for prizes, and music by the popular Hampton Beach concert bands.

In the early years, especially, there was plenty of exhibition airplane flying and parachute jumping—with takeoffs and landings right on the beach. There were planes rides for paying customers and free ones for the winning Carnival Queens.

Over the years, millions of people attended Carnival Week. They came mainly from the mill towns of the Merrimack Valley—places like Haverhill, Lowell, and Lawrence in Massachusetts and Manchester in New Hampshire.

The Queen contest was a main feature of the Carnival. The contestants were young women who sold "popularity vote" tickets at ten to twenty-five cents apiece. With these tickets the Board of Trade gave away new Ford and Chevrolet cars, garages, a beach cottage, and even a cocker spaniel. Whoever sold the most tickets was declared the Carnival Queen and was crowned on an improvised throne near the beach bandstand at the conclusion of an elaborate, costumed Mardi Gras parade down Ocean Boulevard to the front of the Hampton Beach Casino.

In this period there were twenty-six Carnival Queens, the first one crowned in 1915 and the last in 1940. After the period of World War II (1941-1945) contestants returned again to Hampton Beach, not to vie for top honors as ticket sellers, but as true beach beauty queens.

1915 Carnival Queen Blanche Thompson and Massachusetts aviator J. Chauncey Redding at Hampton Beach.

1915—BLANCHE THOMPSON, HAVERHILL MA

In 1915, 50,513 votes were cast at one penny each, the proceeds going to fund entertainment at the beach. The first Carnival Queen was 17-year-old Blanche Thompson of Haverhill, Massachusetts, who raised about $300 "with a little help from her Dad." She received a diamond ring, a heart-shaped box of candy, and an aeroplane ride from J. Chauncey Redding, the first licensed aviator in Massachusetts.

Blanche chose as her king Arthur Ford, whose family owned the Pelham Hotel at the beach. She recalled later in life that she had been crowned by her future sister in law, Marion Evans. The crowning took place at the Hampton Beach Mardi Gras festival on September 9, 1915.

FIRST CARNIVAL WEEK AVIATOR J. CHAUNCEY REDDING

In 1915, with powered flight still in its infancy, an aerial act billed as "the most thrilling ever seen in New England" made daily appearances at the new, end-of-summer Hampton Beach Carnival Week. Capitalizing on the war then being fought in Europe—in which combat aircraft played an important part—aviator J. Chauncey Redding and Somerville ice cream company heir J. Howard Bushway demonstrated the art of "aerial warfare…in which a defended fort is bombarded and destroyed by intrepid aviators high in the air out of reach of the fort's guns." Parachutist Phil Bullman demonstrated the tricky art of jumping out of a perfectly good airplane. When Blanche was crowned Queen of the Carnival, Redding took her aloft for the thrill of a lifetime. Later in life she recalled to local reporters the excitement of flying up to 1,000 feet and then landing on the sands of Hampton Beach with a flat tire.

1916—MRS. CLARA DUDLEY, HAMPTON BEACH NH

1916 Carnival Queen Mrs. Clara Dudley.

At least nine women entered the contest this year, including three married ones, selling tickets for a chance to win the new Ford automobile on display at the Casino bowling alley. The King of the Carnival, Kenneth French of Boston, arrived on Labor Day and was presented with the keys to the beach by the Board of Trade, after which he would have "the full freedom…of the gaily decorated seashore city." Three days later, French and the top ticket seller, Mrs. Clara Dudley of Hampton Beach, were crowned at the Mardi Gras festivities, attended by an estimated 20,000 people. Second place was awarded to Constance Johnson of South Groveland, Massachusetts; third to Irene Garland of Manchester, New Hampshire; fourth to Hattie Higgins of Exeter; and fifth to Myrtle Lamprey of Hampton. The Hampton Beach Board of Trade presented Clara with a diamond ring and a bouquet of flowers, and aviator Farnum Fish treated her to an airplane ride, of which she "expressed her experience as delightful." The second and third place winners also received "diamond rings of value." R. J. Donahue of Dorchester, Massachusetts held the winning ticket to the Ford automobile that was given away in the contest.

EARLY BEACH PIONEER CLARA DUDLEY

Clara was the wife of Hampton Beach Board of Trade member Joseph S. Dudley. Around the turn of the 20th century the couple came from Massachusetts to set up a tintype photography shop in a tent on the corner of C Street and Ocean Boulevard. They later went into partnership with fellow beach business pioneers Joseph and Daisy White, and together they ran Dudley and White, a combination photography studio and variety store. They added White's Café, which became one of the most popular eating places on the New Hampshire seacoast. The store the Dudleys operated at the time of Joe's death in 1942 was located on the original site, and is still owned by members of the Dudley family.

THE BOY AVIATOR FARNUM FISH

The 1915 Carnival Week aviators Redding and Bullman had been an immediate and memorable hit, and had they survived when their plane crashed into a Saugus, Massachusetts marsh a month later, they likely would have been back the following year. J. Howard Bushway instead procured the 19-year-old "Boy Aviator," whose daring aerial exploits, not the least of which was being shot at and wounded while flying a scouting mission for Pancho Villa in the Mexican Revolution, were all the current rage. "Nine months actual experience with Villa's army in Mexico!" trumpeted the exhibition advertisements.

This early war pilot and barnstormer was Farnum Thayer Fish of Los Angeles, California, the world's youngest licensed aviator. He had earned his pilot's certificate at age fifteen, after completing four hours of flight instruction with aviation pioneer Orville Wright at the Wrights' flying school in Dayton, Ohio. Farnum quoted Orville as saying, "If you couldn't learn to fly in four hours, you shouldn't be flying anyway." This suited Farnum's need for speed, and he immediately bought a Wright Model B biplane, shipped it home, and entered what the Wright brothers had called the "mountebank business"—exhibition flying.

Fish was born and raised in California, but his namesakes had been New Englanders. The first Farnum Fish, born in 1775 in Uxbridge, Massachusetts, settled in Swanzey, New Hampshire, where he married Rachel Thayer, a physician's daughter. Their third son was the Boy Aviator's grandfather, Ezra Thayer Fish, who went on to make his fortune in Pennsylvania coal. Ezra's son Charles, a physician, left the weathery East in favor of sunny southern California, where he married Catherine Goodfellow and raised two boys, Winthrop and Farnum.

Farnum's most interesting relation was his maternal uncle Dr. George Emory Goodfellow, a gutsy, perpetual motion machine, an expert on gunshot wounds and a pioneer in the use of sterile techniques. He kept an office above the Crystal Palace

Saloon in Tombstone, Arizona so he could gamble and drink when he wasn't pulling bullets out of cowboys and lawmen like Virgil and Morgan Earp of O.K. Corral fame. Among his many exploits, he hunted and then befriended the Apache warrior Goyahkla (Geronimo), got himself bitten by a Gila monster to see if its venom was as poisonous as was commonly believed (it wasn't, but it still kicked like a mule), and survived the disastrous 1906 San Francisco earthquake.

"Hair-Raising Stunts Performed by Birdmen in Rattle Traps"

This early headline exemplified the adventurous, restless spirit of the times that had Doc Goodfellow's nephew firmly in its thrall. Before discovering the thrill of piloting his own "rattle trap," Farnum channeled the zeitgeist into petty law-breaking. As an aviator he was at times suspended and blacklisted for not following the rules. He enjoyed performing dare-devilish, dangerous feats like the Death Dip and Texas Tommy Twist for his earthbound spectators. He also liked to "mushroom hunt" (fly low) over the tops of their heads, which got him into trouble with aviation officials on more than one occasion.

Aviators J. Howard Bushway (left) and Farnum Fish exhibited at Hampton Beach during the 1916 Carnival Week. Fish gave Carnival Queen Clara Dudley a ride in his machine.

A combination of skilled aerial showman and a cat with nine lives, Farnum had survived some pretty hairy crashes into a pond in Wisconsin and the ocean at Revere Beach in Massachusetts. In June 1916, he performed flawlessly over the Charles River Basin in Boston, but at neighboring Lynn the following month, as he was attempting his signature bomb-dropping stunt, several of the homemade devices detonated in the plane's bomb box beneath the passenger seat. His assistant received burns when his shoes and clothes caught fire, but Farnum was able to land the plane safely. At the Nashua, New Hampshire fairgrounds a few weeks later he attempted to take off from the infield of the track as a motorcycle race was in progress. The airplane snagged on the fence at the far end of the field and crashed onto the track as "nine motorcyclists were tearing around it." Farnum received burns to his face and wrist and his parachutist Joe Schiber suffered several sprains, but they skirted any serious damage.

As promised, in September 1916 Farnum T. Fish, billed as the "Latest in Aviation," appeared at Hampton Beach. For his Carnival Week debut he gave "one of the most successful aeroplane flights of the week, reaching a high altitude." In a time when the public could only read about the European war they would soon be fighting in, he gave them visual "demonstrations of aerial bombardment and of the various capabilities of the flying machine in time of war." After the bombing runs came the parachute jumps. The parachutist's first fall out of the plane put him "near I Street," but in landing he fell and was injured. Not too badly, as his jump the following day was reported to have been "finely executed."

Like Chauncey Redding the year before, Farnum took the Carnival Queen for a ride in the sky. With her long skirts safely roped down, Clara enjoyed a "long trip to the southerly part of the beach," and returned to circle the Casino before landing.

It may have been a wishful guesstimate, but it was reported that a single day's attendance "easily" totaled 100,000—all on hand to cheer Farnum's aerial maneuvers over Hampton Beach. If the numbers are true, his Carnival Week appearance was the high water mark in his career as a stunt aviator. He had exhibited in front of huge crowds before, but this may have been his largest ever.

On stage in front of the Hampton Beach bandstand, 1917 Carnival Queen Madeline Higgins with King of the Carnival Albert Kranz and his "bold, bad pirate gang."

1917—MADELINE HIGGINS, HAVERHILL MA

Depending on the newspaper report, in 1917 the King of the Carnival, Albert Kranz of Amesbury, Massachusetts, sailed into Hampton Beach "in all his regal robes and surrounded by a bold, bad pirate gang," saluted from shore by "aerial bombs and the cheers of a great Labor Day crowd," or he arrived at the scene in a "gaily decorated automobile." By whatever conveyance he made his initial appearance, Kranz received the keys to the beach and the invitation to "rule supreme" over Carnival Week. A "parade of bathing girls" had preceded his arrival. The winner of the parade was Ruth Dow of Haverhill, Massachusetts, who was awarded a prize for having the best bathing costume. Several days later, on September 6, 1917, King Kranz and the young woman who had sold the most popularity vote tickets—Madeline Higgins of Haverhill, Massachusetts—were crowned. Madeline wore the same crown and costume as the 1916 Queen. The ceremony was followed by judging of the best, most original, and most grotesque costumes worn by the Mardi Gras parade participants.

THIS IS

"CARNIVAL COTTAGE"

To be GIVEN AWAY during Carnival Week by the Hampton and Hampton Beach Board of Trade

"The Cottage That Someone Gets for a Dime."

"CARNIVAL COTTAGE"

Is the last cottage on the left as one walks down C Street. It is a well constructed modern cottage, built for the Carnival of 1917 by John Janvrin of Hampton. With each vote purchased in the Queen of the Carnival Contest is given without extra charge a coupon which may win this $800.00 house.

Queen of the Carnival Votes may be purchased of Any Contestant or at Any Store, Hotel, or Business Place

BUY YOURS TODAY

The Dime you spend may Win a Summer Home

8

In 1917 the Hampton Beach Board of Trade gave away a "Carnival Cottage" using the Carnival Queen popularity vote tickets, a legal sleight of hand that allowed the Board to skirt the state's lottery laws.

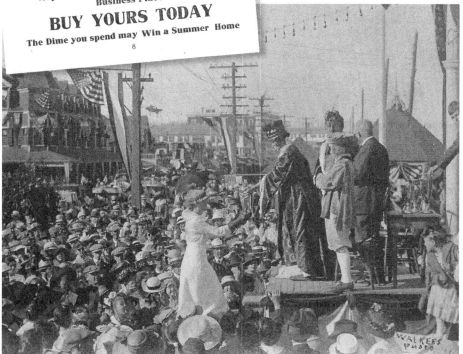

Carnival Queen Madeline Higgins at the bandstand awarding trophies to the winners of the decorated automobile contest during the 1917 Carnival Week.

1918—ADELINE STEVENS, HAMPTON NH

The 1918 Labor Day celebration at Hampton Beach was named the Red Cross Carnival, with Carnival Queen contestants soliciting funds for the Red Cross's World War I relief efforts. The girl who garnered the most funds was Adeline Stevens, a Hampton Academy student and daughter of English-born trolley operator Lewis F. Stevens of Hampton. Adeline was crowned queen on September 8, 1918.

Adeline Stevens (center) as a Hampton Academy student in 1915.

Lewis F. Stevens, c. 1915, a trolley starter, conductor, and for several years the acting superintendent of the Exeter, Hampton, and Amesbury street railway.

1918

WE NEED YOU

Red Cross parade float at Hampton Beach, 1918 or 1919.

1919—MAE ASH, LAWRENCE MA

The Labor Day Carnival was called the Victory Carnival this year, in honor of the armistice signed on November 11, 1918 to end World War I. Each day of the Carnival was named for one of the victorious countries, and the boulevard was decorated and renamed "The Victory Avenue of the Allies." Mae Ash of Lawrence, Massachusetts was the top ticket seller in the Carnival Queen contest and she chose as her king Bill Bigley, the

1919 Carnival Queen and King, May Ash and Bill Bigley.

hotshot hitter for the beach baseball team, whose family ran the Olympia Theatre. They were crowned at the Mardi Gras on September 8, 1919. The Board of Trade gave away a new Ford automobile to the holder of the winning Carnival Queen ticket.

Carnival Queen May Ash awarding a soldier at the Hampton Beach bandstand, September 1919.

Bill Bigley with the Hampton Beach baseball team, 1922.

1919

1920—LULU ROBERTS, EXETER NH

In 1920 some local church groups complained about the Board of Trade's lottery-style contest to give away a new automobile. After the state attorney general declared it illegal, the Rockingham County solicitor stopped the sale of tickets by the Carnival Queen contestants. Even so, a winner was selected, Lulu Roberts of Exeter, New Hampshire. She chose as her king Leslie McKay, also of Exeter. They were crowned at the conclusion of the costumed Mardi Gras parade down the boulevard to the bandstand in front of the Casino on September 11, 1920.

1921—FRANCES FAY FORD, BRIGHTON MA

In 1921 the Carnival Queen contestants sold official programs instead of car raffle tickets, and were joined by men who wished to vie for the title of Carnival King (not many did, and the men's contest was not continued). The top program sellers were Frances Fay Ford of Hampton Beach and Brighton, Massachusetts and Harry Waters of Dorchester, Massachusetts. They were crowned at the Mardi Gras on September 10, 1921.

The Carnival was billed as "7 Aladdin-Like Days and Nights," with Daredevil Van Norman as the headliner. Featured this year was "The Pageant of Hampton," billed as a "historical and allegorical presentation by means of tableaux and pantomime of outstanding incidents which occurred in the early days of this ancient town…the entire town will participate in the staging of the pageant on the white sands of the famous Hampton Beach each evening during the entire Carnival week."

With his "ride of death," Daredevil Van Norman headlined at the 1921 Carnival Week.

Reverend Ira and Vina Jones dressed for parts in a Hampton historical pageant, c. 1925. Both were instrumental in forming the town's historical society, The Meetinghouse Green Memorial and Historical Association, now known as the Hampton Historical Society.

In 1921 WWI aviator Jack Blake flew stunts and passengers over the beach in Bob Fogg's silver Merrimack. He and his mechanic were called upon to drop inflated tubes down to bathers trapped in an undertow at White Rocks near the mouth of the Hampton River. All were saved except a 15-year-old girl who drowned.

Bob Fogg's Merrimack *at Hampton Beach, 1921.*

1922—CONSTANCE BLOCK, NORTH HAMPTON NH

1
9
2
2

This year's Carnival Queen contestants sold ten-cent tickets for a chance to win a new Ford sedan. Constance Block of North Hampton, New Hampshire, was the winner, having sold $1,100 worth of tickets. She chose Frank Hobbs, also of North Hampton, as her king. They were crowned on September 9, 1922, at the closing celebration of Carnival Week. The "Spirit of Hampton," another historical pageant based on Hampton's early history, was performed by members of the community during Carnival Week.

One of the earliest beach beauty contests was held in July at Armas Guyon's Dance Carnival, located on Boar's Head at the north end of Hampton Beach. The judges, which included Harlan "Pink" Baker, "Princeton's famous all-around athlete," passed out red cards to twenty-five girls whom they considered the prettiest in the hall. The winner was Margaret O'Rourke of the Elizabeth Cottage, who won the title of "Miss Hampton" and received a silver loving cup as a prize.

Hampton Beach street scene, looking south along Ocean Boulevard, c. 1925. The building at left is the combined Police and Comfort Station, built in 1921.

1923—BERTHA DUPLEISSIS, MANCHESTER NH

As in 1917, the Board of Trade again raffled off a carnival cottage. This year they offered a five-room "portable" house worth several thousand dollars, which they managed to squeeze into place between the entertainment stage and the police station. Contractors plumbed and electrified the house, and the Atherton-Peoples Furniture Company of Haverhill, Massachusetts furnished it. Carnival Queen contestants sold 25 cent admission tickets for a tour of the interior of the cottage, although the Board of Trade hardly bothered to disguise the fact that the price of admission also bought a chance to win the house. The winning ticket holder would have to move the prize to his or her own lot, at an estimated cost of $100.

LADIES DESIRING TO ENTER THE
QUEEN OF THE CARNIVAL CONTEST
APPLY TO SECRETARY   Office, Opposite Casino
Lady Selling Largest Number of Admission Tickets Will be the Queen
LIBERAL PRIZES FOR ALL CONTESTANTS

The 1923 Carnival Cottage on the beach between the entertainment stage and the Police Station. It was later moved to C Street and was a private residence for many years.

The presence of the carnival cottage was not welcomed by everyone. "Do You Know," jibed Jim Tucker, editor of the Hampton Beach News-Guide, "that many beach residents believe that the town authorities are absolutely wrong in allowing a summer house to occupy a choice space on the beachfront merely because the house happens to be mounted on wheels and is propelled by a gasoline engine?"

Despite grumblings that the house took up too much prime real estate at the height of the summer season, it remained in place on the beach. The ladies continued to sell their tickets, even enlisting family and friends to help. The winner was Bertha Dupleissis of Manchester, who chose as her king James Coffey of Portsmouth.

At the close of Carnival Week the winning ticket was drawn in the name of T. W. Litchfield of Lexington, Massachusetts. Either this cottage or the one raffled in 1917 became Farr's Fried Chicken on C Street, after serving as a summer cottage for many years (the present building's L-shape favors the 1923 cottage as the correct one).

Farr's Famous Fried Chicken shack in 2016.

1924—MILDRED DUDLEY, HAMPTON BEACH NH

The top ticket seller in the Carnival Queen contest this year was Mildred Dudley, a Hampton Academy student and daughter of the 1916 Queen, Clara Dudley. Her king was Louis Boudreau of Camp Devens, Mass. Their coronation was "witnessed by fully 30,000 persons." For her win Mildred received a trip to New York City, to be accompanied by "a chaperone of her own choosing." She later married orchestra musician Arne Autio and ran Dudley's Hotel, Gift Shop, and Tea Room at the beach.

1924 Carnival Queen Mildred Dudley.

Miss New England. In 1924 the Board of Trade conducted a photo contest to "pick the most beautiful bathing girl" at the beach. From the reported 150 entrant pictures taken by local photographer Dave Colt, the lone judge, artist E. Wyatt Kimball, chose as the winner 17-year-old Bernice Rand of Exeter, New Hampshire. Along with the title of Miss New England, she received a silver "Neptune's Daughter Loving Cup." The runners-up were all Massachusetts girls: second place Miss Ahearn of Cambridge, third place Anna McDonald of Lynn, and fourth place Velma Shales of Worcester.

1924

TO GIVE WONDERFUL SILVER LOVING CUP TO PRETTIEST BATHING QUEEN AT HAMPTON

"Neptune's Daughter" Trophy, Valued at $100, to be Presented at Big Bathing Pageant in August. Photographs Taken Without Charge and Submitted to Group of Eminent Artists for Judging.

WINNER TO BE CALLED "MISS NEW ENGLAND"

In 1924 Miss New England was chosen by photograph only. A beauty pageant of the same name was held at the beach from 1956 to 1965.

1925—BOBBIE ROWELL, HAMPTON NH

Bobbie Rowell, an employee at the Mason Dry Goods store in Hampton, won this year's Carnival Queen contest, which featured as raffle prizes a Ford Tudor sedan and a garage built by the Davis-Watson Manufacturing Company of Nashua, New Hampshire. She was crowned at the conclusion of the "Coronation Mardi Gras Parade" on September 11, 1925. As Mrs. Warren Cann, she would compete and win again in 1939.

Miss New England. Started last year, the bathing beauty contest was held again in 1925. The winner was Hazel Houghton of Lowell, Massachusetts, whose prize was a large silver loving cup. After the awards ceremony the bathing beauties paraded along Ocean Boulevard, from the open air stage opposite the Hampton Beach Casino to C Street and back again, led by clown performer "rube cop" Bill Reno and Hal McDonnell's band (which had performed at the bandstand twice a day throughout the summer).

The 1925 Carnival Week prize garage.

Junior bathing beauty winner, eight-year-old Virginia Calnan of Lowell MA.

1925 Miss New England Hazel Houghton of Lowell MA (left). Dorothy Dobbins of Methuen MA (right) took second place.

The Carnival Queens 1915-1940

Stunt rider Allo Diavolo performed at Carnival Week in 1925.

The popular Hal McDonnell Band of Haverhill MA played at the bandstand in the 1920s and again in the 1940s.

Bathing beauties at Hampton Beach in 1925.

1926—MARION GILMORE, EXETER NH

King and Queen of the 1926 Carnival, William Cooper and Marion Gilmore.

In 1926 the Board of Trade debuted the popular pageant character of King Neptune, played by Edward Uhlig of Manchester, New Hampshire, who would reign over the Carnival, and with trident in hand crown the winning Queen and her chosen consort.

The Queen contestants sold tickets for a chance to win a Ford roadster. Marion Gilmore of Exeter, New Hampshire was the top ticket seller. As noted by a purple prosed newspaper reporter, on September 10, 1926, Marion and her chosen king William Cooper, also of Exeter, were crowned "by the hand of King Neptune, who conferred upon their brows the crowns emblematic of their high positions… amid a spectacle of royalty, purple robes, speckled with confetti and emblazoned by powerful arc lights." Hazel Armington of Nashua, New Hampshire took second place. Her prince was James Kelley of Lawrence, Massachusetts. As in previous years, a costume contest followed the Mardi Gras coronation, with Mildred Dudley of Hampton Beach, representing "winter," winning the prize for "prettiest" costume. Charles Eastman, an employee of White's Café at Hampton Beach, held the winning ticket for the Ford roadster.

Historical pageant fever descended upon the beach again in 1926. This year's theme was based on the story of off-kilter Hampton patriot Edward Gove, played by local police officer Bill Elliot, whose rebellion against the English government in the early 1680s never quite got off the ground (he is nevertheless seated prominently among the pantheon of Hampton's early heroes).

Bunny and Walter White, the children of Hampton Beach business owners John and Daisy White, ready to compete in the decorated automobile contest at Carnival Week (1926).

1927—CHARLOTTE BRISTOL, HAMPTON NH

The Hampton Beach Board of Trade was now called the Hampton and Hampton Beach Chamber of Commerce. Its directors voted to award a Chevrolet automobile to the holder of the winning Carnival Queen ticket. They also voted to begin the Carnival Queen contest earlier in the summer season, on July 15, and to award the winner an all-expenses-paid, ten-day trip through Georgia, "in addition to the usual coronation festivities on Friday night of Carnival week which will be held on a more elaborate scale than ever this year."

Charlotte Bristol of Hampton won Carnival Queen this year. She chose as her king Walter Farrell of Lowell, Massachusetts. Following the coronation on September 9, a masked costume ball

This costumed woman has been identified as Charlotte Bristol of Hampton.

was held in the newly-constructed Hampton Beach Casino Ballroom. It was reported that "the queen and her suite were the guests of the evening, and were feted by the thousands of visitors and residents of the beach."

As the second place winner, Mildred Dudley (Carnival Queen of 1924) was awarded the title of "crown princess." Her ball escort was John McDonnell of Cambridge, Massachusetts. Third place went to Madeline Sherwood of Haverhill, Massachusetts.

1
9
2
7

1928—MAE FOUNTAIN, LAWRENCE MA

On September 7, 1928, a crowd of 10,000 jammed the boulevard for the Carnival Week Mardi Gras festivities. The parade started at the Ross Garage, led by the Hampton police, Hal McDonnell's band, and a float carrying the top ticket seller, Carnival Queen-elect Mae Fountain of Lawrence, Massachusetts and her "royal consort" Ken Langley of Hampton. In what was now a traditional ceremony, King Neptune performed the crowning at the bandstand. Second place went to Evelyn Clark of North Hampton, New Hampshire and third to Doris Stevens of Lawrence, Massachusetts. The Chamber of Commerce presented a diamond ring to each of the three winners.

A Mardi Gras costume contest followed the coronation, and was itself followed by a second costume contest, held indoors at the Casino Ballroom. Accompanied by the music of Hughie Connor's Bancroft Hotel Orchestra, the costumed contestants took several turns around the ballroom as they were judged. In the Casino judging, Mildred Dudley of Hampton Beach won Most Beautiful Costume.

Trade card for Hughie Connor and his Bancroft Hotel Orchestra of Worcester, Massachusetts.

1929—DORIS SPACKMAN, PORTSMOUTH NH

"King Karnival and his Kourt" opened Carnival Week on September 2, 1929. Doris Spackman of Portsmouth, New Hampshire was the top ticket seller in the Carnival Queen contest, and she was crowned at the Mardi Gras festivities held on September 6. Her "attendants" were second place Bernice Bartlett of Lawrence, Massachusetts; third place Gertrude Campbell of Manchester, New Hampshire; and fourth place Helen Dugan of Belmont, Massachusetts.

Two new features were added to Carnival Week this year: a horse show staged in the lot behind the Casino and a "$6000 Out-of-Door Concert Electrola" that broadcast concerts and announcements from a "singing tower" above the Chamber of Commerce building on the beachfront. Also featured was a "realistic and amusing sketch" called "Fighting the Flames," in which a tall building burst into flames, antics ensued, and a woman jumped from the upper story into a life net. Advertising for the event assured potential spectators that "the fire department succeeds in controlling the flames, but the entire exhibition is full of thrills."

THE ORTHOPHONIC VICTROLA BY JAMES TUCKER

(Excerpt from James Tucker's 'Our Town' column, Hampton Union, March 13, 1952).

In the late 1920s, the Chamber of Commerce purchased from John Hassett in Portsmouth, an Orthophonic Victrola with a gigantic loud speaker which was constructed of wood and was at least seven feet square. The speaker was mounted on a low, wheeled truck and placed in a square tower built on top of the Chamber office.

The tower had casement windows on all four sides which could be opened wide to allow the great orthophonic speaker to be wheeled into any position. Records or radio could be played through the speaker or voice announcements made by means of a microphone. Eventually, microphones were placed in the bandstand in order that concerts by the band could be broadcast over the beach through the speaker which was placed usually in the door on the north side of the tower.

In 1930, a small stage was built about two feet above ground level on the north side of the Chamber office and covered with an awning. The stage, which resembled a veranda, was equipped with a piano and a microphone. Here, the first Monday night auditions were held and it was on this stage, as we remember it, that Bill Elliot, Hampton's famous "Singing Cop," learned microphone technique and got a big start on his way to radio and concert popularity.

With the continuing improvement and refinement of what are now called "sound systems," there have been many changes in these facilities at Hampton Beach, but those of us who were associated with it, will never forget the original Orthophonic Victrola.

Postcard of Hampton Beach, c. 1930. "Orthophonic Electrola and Radio" concerts and announcements were broadcast from the "singing tower" above the Chamber of Commerce building on the left. The prize automobile for which the Carnival Queen contestants sold tickets can be seen to the left of the building.

1930—DOROTHY DUDLEY, HAMPTON BEACH NH

1930 Carnival Queen Dorothy Dudley.

The 1930 Carnival Week featured an automobile show and "circus flying" by planes from the Hampton Airport. Sundown, a Seneca chief and Dartmouth college student, "whose appearance with the Big Green football team in numerous stadia throughout the East created a real sensation," sang at the bandstand with Hal McDonnell's Hampton Beach band.

Hampton businessman Thomas Cogger directed the Queen of the Carnival contest this year. Contestants sold tickets for a new Chevrolet car, won by William Cash of Hampton. This year's Carnival Queen was Dorothy Dudley, crowned on September 5, 1930. She was the daughter of Clara Dudley who had won in 1916, and the younger sister of Mildred Dudley who had won in 1924.

This Dudley dynasty of beach queens can trace its origins to husband and father Joseph S. Dudley, one of the pioneer businessmen at Hampton Beach. Around the turn of the 20th century Joe became intrigued by the tourism opportunities of a beach that boasted a first rate trolley system and a spacious new Casino. He and his wife Clara set up a tintype photography business in a tent on the corner of C Street and Ocean Boulevard. The store they operated at the time of Joe's death in 1942 was located on the same site, which is still owned by members of the Dudley family.

Dorothy was crowned amid the same carnival atmosphere as her mother fourteen years earlier. Later, as Mrs. Dorothy Cheney, she owned and operated a clothing and gift shop in the Seagate Hotel on Ashworth Avenue. Her daughter Carole Wheeler *(see page 57)* continued the family tradition by competing in the 1952-1954 Miss Hampton Beach and other pageants.

1930

1931—EDITH WEBSTER, HAMPTON BEACH NH

On September 6, 1931, the Carnival Queen crowning ceremony took the form of a "Hindoo pageant" with a "stern grand vizier," played by J. Frank James of the Chamber of Commerce, and the King, Lawrence Tucker of Hampton, "garbed in elaborate rajah costume." Along with "harem girls," a "beautiful dancing slave girl," and a "master of slaves," Hal McDonnell's band led the Mardi Gras parade from Ross Garage to a stage near the bandstand where the grand vizier crowned the king and queen.

To win her title, Carnival Queen Edith Webster—who was "very beautiful in sparkling white"—had sold a total of 79,305 votes. As reported by the Haverhill Gazette, it was the "first time in 17 years that the White Island section of the beach has had one of its daughters on the throne."

Hazel Ireland of Hampton Beach took a dim second place with 27,830 votes. Patricia Collins of Cambridge, Massachusetts came in third with 25,420 votes.

Besides awarding a new automobile to winning ticket holder James Fitzgerald of Haverhill, Massachusetts, the Chamber of Commerce gave away a cocker spaniel, won by Monica Callahan of Lawrence, Massachusetts.

"Buy Carnival Queen Votes Here." Postcard of Hampton Beach in the early 1930s.

1932—MABEL FITZGERALD, SALISBURY MA

A weekly radio audition contest for aspiring singers was held at the beach during the 1932 summer season. The final contest was broadcast during Carnival Week over the Chamber of Commerce "singing tower." A medieval court graced the Mardi Gras festivities, with a presiding "English Bishop" played by J. Frank James of the Chamber. "Despite cold weather and a run of high tide," on September 9, 1932, James crowned the new Queen of the Hampton Beach Carnival, Mabel Fitzgerald of Salisbury, Massachusetts. Mabel chose as her king Lee Burbridge of Hampton, and her attendants were the second through fifth place winners—Charlotte Eaton of Seabrook, New Hampshire, Irene Cahill; Helen Marsh; and Hazel Nichols. C. G. Bates of the North Beach section of Hampton Beach won the Chevrolet car, and Thomas Badger of Somerville, Massachusetts won an electric clock.

1933—PHYLLIS TUCKER, HAMPTON BEACH NH

The medieval court was again the theme for this year's Mardi Gras. On September 8, 1933, "one of the most beautiful nights of the whole season," J. Frank James reprised his role as the English Bishop to crown the Carnival Queen winner, Phyllis Tucker of Hampton Beach. Phyllis, an employee of the Cozy Corner Cafe, chose as her king Woodrow Foss of Haverhill, Massachusetts. Second place Virginia Dennett of Hampton was named Princess, with her future husband Carl Dining of Stratham as the Prince. The Chamber presented a diamond ring to Phyllis and a wrist watch to Virginia. Last year's winner, Mabel Fitzgerald, also received a diamond ring.

1933 Carnival Queen Phyllis Tucker (1930). *1933 Carnival Princess Virginia Dennett (1935).*

In 1937, Phyllis, her father James Tucker, and newsman William Cram founded The Society in Hampton Beach for the Apprehension of Those Falsely Accusing Eunice "Goody" Cole of Having Familiarity With the Devil, *and in 1938 she played the part of the persecuted Goody Cole for Hampton's 300th anniversary celebration. Left: Phyllis as Goody Cole in a pillory (1938).*

1934—BLANCHE HAMILTON, ORANGE MA

1934 Carnival Queen Blanche Hamilton.

No doubt the most talented of the 26 Hampton Beach Carnival Queens was New England Conservatory of Music student Blanche Hamilton of Orange, Massachusetts. She played violin and piano, taught violin classes, and was the business manager of *Neume,* the Conservatory's yearbook.

Blanche chose John Kelly, a former Bowdoin College athlete, as her Carnival King. On September 7, 1934, they were crowned at the Carnival Week Mardi Gras festivities. Second place Mary Grandmaison of Haverhill, Massachusetts and third place Lucille Grandmaison of Hampton Beach served as attendants.

Vaudeville entertainers at the Hampton Beach bandstand in the 1930s.

Club Cascades Revue and the Hal McDonnell Band featured in the 1935 Carnival Week Souvenir Program.

1935—CATHERINE SARGENT, HAMPTON NH

In August 1935 the Chamber of Commerce again conducted weekly radio auditions for aspiring singers, with the final round held during Carnival Week. Bill Elliot, who got his start with the auditions, was now a soloist with the beach band.

The top ticket seller in the Carnival Queen contest was Catherine Sargent, a Hampton Academy sophomore. On September 6, 1935, with a colonial theme to mark this year's Mardi Gras, J. Frank James as King Neptune crowned Catherine and her chosen king, William Fitzgerald of Manchester, New Hampshire. The Queen's "ladies in waiting" were the Jones sisters of Boston, Massachusetts; Helen Barron of Haverhill, Massachusetts; Beatrice Wells of Hampton Beach; and Rita Daley of Arlington, Massachusetts.

Appearing as costumed "gentlemen of the court" were George Dunn of Melrose, Massachusetts; Robert Carr of Milton, Massachusetts; Robert Kiley of Newbury, Vermont; and Roy Sargent of Hampton Beach. The arrival of the queen was announced by the pages Augusta Dubrack and Leona Carter, both of Seabrook, New Hampshire.

1935

Spanish Colonial Revival architecture, south end of the Hampton Beach Casino, home to the Ballroom, Market, and Automatic Dreamland Arcade, c. 1935. With construction started in 1927, the Ballroom opened for dancing in April 1928.

1936—PAULINE WHITEHOUSE, HAVERHILL MA

The 36-year-old beach bandstand was improved with a stage and speakers this year. Vacationists cast their Carnival Queen votes nearby, at a booth at the Chamber of Commerce office. Mrs. Ethel Powers Uhlig, who directed the annual Children's Day festivities, now directed the Carnival Queen pageant. Pauline Whitehouse of Haverhill, Massachusetts won the Carnival Queen contest, and she chose as her king John Haggerty of Nashua, New Hampshire. On September 11, 1936, they were crowned at the Mardi Gras festivities by J. Frank James of the Chamber of Commerce.

1937 Carnival Queen Delores Gauron

1937—DELORES GAURON, HAMPTON BEACH NH

With a total of 54,980 votes cast in her favor, Hampton Academy student Dolores Gauron won Carnival Queen this year. She was reported to be (at the time) the youngest queen in the contest's history. With 41,600 votes, Pauline DelaBarre of Alliston, Massachusetts came in second. Dolores chose as her king Albert Mills of Haverhill. Their crowning—by outgoing monarchs Pauline Whitehouse and John Haggerty—took place on September 10, 1937 "with colorful pageantry, reminiscient of the Shakespearian era," and with "tiny" Lois Yell of Hampton, who in 1947 would win Miss Cover Girl, as the flower girl. Charles Butler of the Chamber of Commerce presented diamond rings to the winning girls. The Mardi Gras that year included a stage show called "Midnight in Paris," and songs by local favorite Bill Elliot.

1937 Carnival Princess Pauline Delabarre

1938—DOROTHY MITCHELL, HAMPTON NH

The town of Hampton celebrated its 300th anniversary this year, with parades, pageants, and historical events to mark the milestone. Both beach and town experienced an unprecedented crush of visitors well into September.

Dorothy Mitchell of Hampton garnered the most votes in the Carnival Queen contest, beating out Vinnie Waite of Lawrence, Massachusetts and Helen Kennedy of Exeter, New Hampshire. Due to the tercentenary events, the Chamber of Commerce canceled the traditional coronation, and instead awarded each contestant a "suitable" prize. The Chevrolet automobile prize was won by Margaret Carrigg of Methuen, Massachusetts.

1
9
3
8

Route 1 billboard announcing Hampton's 300th birthday in 1938.

Betty Tobey (right) was named "Miss Hampton," the queen of the town's tercentenary celebration. Shirley Arnold (left) as runner up was named "Miss Columbia." Both girls were from Hampton.

Portsmouth, New Hampshire architect M.E. Witmer designed the Hampton Beach Casino's futuristic Art Deco facade for Hampton's 300th Anniversary Exposition, held at the Casino, July 4 through September 10, 1938. Left: Artist's sketch of the Casino Tower. Right: Artist's sketch of facade. Below: The 1938 Tercentenary parade at Hampton Beach.

The Casino Tower survived the Long Island Express hurricane of September 21, 1938. It was likely removed from the Casino the following year.

1939—BOBBY ROWELL CANN, HAMPTON BEACH NH

This year marked the silver anniversary of the Carnival Queen contest. The August 24, 1939 issue of the Hampton Union reported that "for the first time in many years a young matron aspires for the honor usually accorded to a single girl. Mrs. Bobbie [Rowell] Cann of the beach is competing against Miss Ethel Hurd of Portsmouth for the carnival honor which will be bestowed during the Carnival Week to follow Labor Day."

The top ticket seller was Bobbie Cann, a mother of three small children. Crowned on September 9, 1939, it was her second time atop the throne—she had won the Carnival Queen contest as a single girl in 1925. For this year's win the Chamber of Commerce awarded her a hefty $100 cash prize, and she in turn presented the gift automobile to the winning ticket holder, Evelyn Dugan of Lawrence, Massachusetts.

HAMPTON BEACH

Expresses

APPRECIATION

To

Maj. Everett Allyn Moses

Conductor of the Famous

Hampton Beach Concert Band

To the Entire

BAND PERSONNEL

To

"Bill" Elliot

The Popular "Singing Cop"

To

Patsy Murray

And to all Other Assisting

Guest Artists

for the most successful season—musically and otherwise—ever experienced at

Happy Hampton

Maj. Everett Allyn Moses
Conductor

"Bill" Elliot
"Hampton's Famous Singing Cop"

Major Everett Moses of St. Petersburg, Florida conducted the Hampton Beach Concert Band in 1939 and 1940. Bill Elliot of Hampton sang with the band.

1940—KATHRYN SULLIVAN, MEDFORD MA

The top ticket seller this year was 21-year-old Kathryn Sullivan of Medford, Massachusetts, who had been coming to the beach with her family for many years. During the war years she had charge of the "war bond booth" at the beach.

Last year's winner Bobbie Rowell Cann took second place in the Queen contest, with Charlotte Moore of Salisbury, Massachusetts taking third.

As it turned out, September 6, 1940 was the last time a Carnival Queen was crowned at the beach.

GALA WEEK AND VICTORY WEEK
1941-1945

Gala Week and Victory Week 1941-1945

In 1941 the Labor Day carnival was renamed Gala Week. The Japanese attack on Pearl Harbor would not come for another three months, but the country had concluded that entry into the European war was inevitable. With the beach in a somber mood, the Carnival Queen contest was canceled, and there were no more contests until after the war. Instead, women sold tickets to raise money for Bundles for Britain, a relief program that sent aid packages to English families. Doris Bragg of Hampton, the top ticket seller, received a prize for her fund-raising efforts, and the winning ticket holder won a new Chevrolet car.

From 1942 to 1945 the Labor Day celebration was called Victory Week. All programs at the beach were dedicated to the armed forces and the sale of war bonds. With the US entry into the war, Bundles for America now joined with Bundles for Britain and a canteen was set up at the beach to furnish free lunches and cigarettes to all on-duty and visiting servicemen.

In 1942 the threat of enemy ships lurking off the coast prompted the Army to enact dim out restrictions, which, however, "failed to retard business" at the beach. Lights from stores and concessions were veiled with "blue cellophane, old awnings, and boards," and blackout shades allowed the Casino Ballroom to have dancing every night. Business went on as usual, with the exception of the state bathhouse, which remained closed the entire season.

In 1943 the Army lifted its restrictions. The Beach held another Victory Week celebration, which ran from August 30 to September 6, Labor Day. Highlighting the week was a war bond drive, a military parade, a "battle of music" between Army and Navy bands, Algi the Talking Robot, and the usual line up of stage acts. Hal McDonnell's band played every day, with Bill Elliot as soloist as well as emcee for portions of the stage events.

The 1944 Victory Week, which ran from August 27 to September 4, Labor Day, was opened by Mayor Tobin of Boston, who had brought to the beach a Gay '90s review that had played in his city. The sale of war bonds was again the main feature.

The following year brought the long-awaited news of victory. The *Hampton Union* headline of August 16, 1945 proclaimed, "Unrestrained Joy and Reverence Mark End of Second World Conflict. Joyful Celebrations Mark Long Awaited Jap Surrender."

The Queens of Hampton Beach

Residents at the beach and elsewhere greeted the news with uninhibited expressions of joy. In the streets of Portsmouth, "snake dances with servicemen and women" spontaneously appeared, while at the beach stores shuttered and people spilled onto the boulevard in front of the bandstand. "At 7 o'clock on Tuesday evening the announcement that World War II was finally over let loose the largest celebration seen in Hampton in many years. The bedlam lasted far into the night, stopping only because the joyous people became exhausted." As Peter Randall noted in his 1989 history of the town, "Hal McDonnell and his band gave a rousing concert, although the music could hardly be heard over the noise of firecrackers, cheers, and noisemakers. People sang, danced, paraded with wash tubs used as drums, and threw confetti, releasing the emotions stored up after three and a half years of war."

Amphibious military vehicle at Hampton Beach, c. 1940.

Instead of selling raffle tickets in the Carnival Queen contest, during the war women raised funds for the Bundles For Britain and Bundles For America relief programs. Above: Hampton women pack supplies at American Legion Post 35 (1942).

Casino at Night, Hampton Beach, N. H.

THE COVER GIRL YEARS
1946-1947

1946—MARILAN EATON, DURHAM NH

In 1946 Carnival Week returned, its theme this year dedicated to the "Future Development of Hampton Beach." There were the usual games, fireworks, band concerts, and aerial performers, with the addition of a fashion show and a "mystery" auction.

Also this year, Edward Seavey, editor of the Beachcomber summer weekly, announced that his paper would sponsor a swimsuit contest at the bandstand. The Chamber of Commerce helped to promote the contest, open to all girls 16 and over who would be judged on their per-

1946 Miss Cover Girl Marilan Eaton.

sonality and appearance. The winner would be hailed as Miss Cover Girl of 1946.

On August 15, just weeks before the Labor Day Carnival was set to open, sixteen contestants paraded before thousands of spectators and a panel of three judges. Bill Elliot was the master of ceremonies and Hal McDonnell's Hampton Beach band played background music.

The judges trimmed the field to eight, then three. After a final tally they announced the 2nd runner up, Marilyn Sheehan from Arlington, Massachusetts; the 1st runner up, Virginia Stubbs from Cuba; and the winner—Miss Cover Girl of 1946—number ten, 20-year-old Marilan Eaton of Durham, New Hampshire.

Marilan, who worked at the Casino, received a $10 prize, gifts from local merchants, an airplane ride, and a portrait sitting with Lillian Clarke, the well-known Hampton Beach silhouette artist.

1
9
4
6

*The eight finalists in the 1946 Miss Cover Girl contest. L-r: Jean Sheridan, Beverly Denis, Katherine Obuchon, **Marilan Eaton**, Jean Marie Daly, **Marilyn Sheehan**, Althea Adams, **Virginia Stubbs**.*

Hampton Beach silhouette artist Lillian Clarke and husband John Bunker, who ran a popcorn stand on the beach.

Left: Lillian Clarke self-portrait, 1945. Right: John Bunker's portrait, 1967.

1947

1947—LOIS YELL, HAMPTON BEACH NH

On August 21, 1947 the Beachcomber and the Chamber of Commerce again sponsored the Miss Cover Girl beauty contest. Again it was held at the bandstand, with Bill Elliot as emcee and ten contestants vying for the title. The judges, beach boosters Victor Grandmaison, Elsie Underwood, and Al Randall, chose as winner 17-year-old Lois Yell of Hampton Beach. Second place went to Caryl Cadario of Arlington, Massachusetts, with third place taken by Jean Bilodeau of Waltham, Massachusetts.

Like Marilan the year before, Lois was showered with gifts, which also included a portrait sitting for a Lillian Clarke silhouette. Although she no longer sold tickets for a chance to win a new automobile, Miss Cover Girl of 1947 was also named Queen of the Carnival. This tradition would continue into the Bandstand years, beginning with the 1948 Miss Hampton Beach contest.

1947 Miss Cover Girl contestants. L-r: Margaret Jacoby, 16, Pawtucket RI; Virginia Stubbs, 18, Pawtucket RI; **Lois Yell, 17, Hampton Beach;** *Lorraine Doucette, 20, Amesbury MA;* **Caryl Cadario, 16, Arlington MA; Jean Bilodeau, 18, Waltham MA**; *Viola Chapman, 17, Cambridge MA; Constance Fletcher, 17, Kittery ME; Sally McHugh, 21, Lowell MA; Jane Adams, 22, Lawrence MA.*

BILL ELLIOT, PAGEANT EMCEE 1946-1965

Bill Elliot (1905-2007) was known as the "Singing Cop" for his days when he would break from his street duties as a traffic cop at Hampton Beach to belt one out at the bandstand. He was a long time Hampton resident and favorite entertainer at the beach.

In 1916, at age 12, he won the first Amateur Night contest at Hampton Beach. In the 1930s he sang on the Major Bowes Amateur Hour in New York City. Although not his primary occupation, Bill had a successful career as a vocalist.

Beginning with the Miss Cover Girl contest in 1946, Bill was emcee for many of the beach beauty contests.

Bill Elliot with beauty contest winners in the 1950s.

In 1995, 90-year-old Bill Elliot crowned the new Miss Hampton Beach, Stephanie Lussier of Manchester NH.

Band Stand and Beach, Hampton Beach, N. H.

MISS HAMPTON BEACH: AT THE BANDSTAND
1948-1958

It's been said that Miss Hampton Beach is the second oldest beauty pageant in New Hampshire, preceded only by Miss Winnipesaukee, which dates to 1925 (the short-lived and virtually unknown Miss New England bathing beauty contest, held at Hampton Beach for at least two years, 1924-1925, predates both contests). While the 1946 Miss Cover Girl contest is sometimes marked as the beginning of the pageant tradition at Hampton Beach, the first named Miss Hampton Beach contest was not held until 1948.

The 1950s spawned the Golden Age of beauty pageants. The first televised Miss America Pageant was broadcast on live TV in 1954, with 27 million people tuning in to watch. The demand for this kind of entertainment increased over the next several decades, and promoters like John Dineen of the Hampton Beach Casino counted on the contests to draw people to the beach. Well-known personalities like Governor Hugh Gregg of New Hampshire and Hampton Playhouse actress Rowena Burack sat in as judges, and Hampton's "Singing Cop," Bill Elliot, referred to in this era as a radio star and disc jockey, was master of ceremonies for many of the contests.

During the Bandstand years, Miss Hampton Beach was made up of three separate events: the contest, the crowning, and the coronation ball.

—*The Contest.* From 1948 to 1953 the contest was held at the start of Carnival Week, during the Labor Day holiday. In 1954 Carnival Week was replaced with an August Festival, which featured a full slate of weekly beauty contests—with names like *Miss Glamour, Miss Sea Nymph, Miss Sunshine, Miss Mermaid, and Miss August Festival*—all leading up to the grand finale of the Miss Hampton Beach contest. The weekly contests lasted through the 1956 season only, when Miss Hampton Beach was moved to the beginning of the Festival to allow the winner to reign over beach events during the entire month of August.

—*The Crowning.* From 1948 until 1955, the crowning was held a few days after the contest, in the evenings at the bandstand, with music by Chuck Hill and the Hampton Beach Concert Band. Beginning in 1956, the crowning was combined with the Coronation Ball.

—*The Carnival Ball/Coronation Ball.* Starting in 1951, to cap the summer season a Grand Carnival Ball attended by the queen and king was held at the Casino Ballroom. In 1955 the Ball was held in advance of the contest, to allow pageant contestants to appear before the public in all their finery. In 1956 the ball was renamed the Coronation Ball and combined with the crowning ceremony. The

Coronation Ball featured a Grand March by the winners, their escorts, and attendants. Dancing followed the queen's coronation, with music by the Ted Herbert and Bob Bachelder orchestras. The last ball was held in 1967.

THE "VITAL STATISTICS"

In this era it became popular for emcees and reporters to make public the winning girl's bust, waist, and hip measurements—her "vital statistics" as they were called. A director of the Miss America pageant said that it was not men who wanted these numbers, but women who wanted to emulate the winners' proportions in their own body shapes. This set the stage for the feminist protests that challenged beauty contests in the 1970s.

Sonja-Bunty Romer, 1953.

Bill Elliot (left) was the contest emcee for many years. Hampton Beach Casino owner John Dineen (right), helped promote the beauty contests.

MIDNIGHT DANCE ★ ★ ★
HAMPTON *Beach* CASINO
TED HERBERT
and his ORCHESTRA *of* 15
$1.00 PLUS TAX — MIDNIGHT TO 4 A.M.
DANCING EVERY NITE
CARNIVAL WEEK STARTS MONDAY
FIREWORKS — BAND CONCERTS — BIG STAGE ACTS

The 1956 Miss Hampton Beach contest at the bandstand with Bill Elliot as emcee. The winner was #14 Cynthia Fuller of Brighton MA (12th from right). #25 Lyla Moran of Boston MA (7th from left) took second and #15 Sally Ann Freedman of Salem MA (13th from right) was third.

The Queens of Hampton Beach

Contests were for kids, too. In the 1950s a Junior King and Queen of the Beach were chosen during the August Children's Day Festival. In 1958, eleven-year-old Bob Dennett of Hampton was chosen King. Bob was the son of Vernon and Eleanor Palmer Dennett, and the nephew of Carl and Virginia Dennett Dining, who as high school students had all played parts in the crowning of the Carnival Queen in 1933. Bob's queen was Veronica Pinkham, also of Hampton. Together they presided over the Coronation Ball that saw Carolyn Komant of Kittery, Maine crowned Miss Hampton Beach.

1958 Junior King and Queen of the Beach, Bob Dennett and Veronica Pinkham, both from Hampton.

Left: Carl and Virginia Dennett Dining and son, c. 1950. Virginia took second place in the 1933 Carnival Queen contest. Carl was her Prince.

Right: Vernon and Eleanor Palmer Dennett, 1955. Both were members of the 1933 Carnival Queen court.

1948—LORRAINE DOUCETTE, AMESBURY MA

The first named Miss Hampton Beach contest, with judging for beauty, personality, and poise, was held on the afternoon of August 25, 1948, one week before the start of Carnival Week. Although the winner no longer sold tickets to gain the title, she also presided as Queen of the Hampton Beach Carnival. In this inaugural year, all contestants were given "Catalina Miss America" swimsuits to wear during the contest.

1948 Miss Hampton Beach Lorraine Doucette.

From a field of 12 contestants, judges chose as winner Lorraine Doucette of Amesbury, who competed in the 1947 Miss Cover Girl contest. Second place went to Caryl Cadario of Arlington Massachusetts, who placed second in the 1947 Miss Cover Girl contest. Third place went to Dolly Cascone of Lawrence, Massachusetts.

Bill Elliot was the master of ceremonies and Chuck Hill's band provided the musical entertainment. The judges were John Dineen of the Hampton Beach Casino, Patsy Fuller of the Penny Arcade, James Foley of the William James Restaurant, David Lifson, manager of the West Newbury, Massachusetts summer theatre, and an unnamed "representative of the 20th century Fox studios in Hollywood."

The crowning of the winner took place on the evening of September 11, the final day of Carnival Week.

1948 Miss Hampton Beach contestants wearing "Catalina Miss America" swimsuits. Winner Lorraine Doucette on far right. Caryl Cadario is 4th from right.

1949—CARYL CADARIO, ARLINGTON MA

1949 Miss Hampton Beach Caryl Cadario.

Red-haired Caryl Cardario of Arlington, Massachusetts was a graduate of Arlington High School, a student at Westbrook Junior College in Portland, Maine, and she worked summers at Munsey's Restaurant on Hampton Beach. She had placed second in 1947 and 1948 before judges chose her from a field of sixteen contestants in this year's Miss Hampton Beach contest, held on August 30, 1949. Competing with her were Hampton area girls Gretchen Brown of Seabrook, New Hampshire and Claire Warwick and Thelma Stickney, both of Hampton Beach. Chamber of Commerce President Ray Goding presented her with a loving cup and John Dineen of the Casino gave her a bouquet of roses. In her secondary role as Carnival Queen, she presided over the Carnival Week festivities.

Taking second place was Sally Atkinson of Ipswich, Massachusetts, who worked at the Casino coffee shop and had been encouraged to enter the contest by her employer John Dineen. Third place went to Virginia Stubbs of Pawtucket, Rhode Island, who worked at Elsie's Beauty Shop at the beach. Both received cash awards.

The contest was under the direction of Chamber of Commerce photographer George Hagopian. Bill Elliot was master of ceremonies and Chuck Hill's band provided the musical entertainment. The judges were John Dineen of the Hampton Beach Casino, James Foley of the William James Restaurant, John Dignon, Rolly Rogers of the Rogers Model Agency in Boston, and models Patti Palmer and Brik Tone.

1
9
4
9

1950—SALLY ATKINSON, IPSWICH MA

After placing second in 1949, Sally Atkinson of Ipswich, Massachusetts took home the top honors this year. Newspaper reports of the pageant, held on August 22, 1950, described her as "beautiful, blue-eyed and blond" and clad in a "lime one-piece suit."

Second place went to Betty Marshall, 20, of Brookline, Massachusetts, with third place going to Barbara McLeod, 19, of Portsmouth, New Hampshire. Also competing were local girls Janis Wright of Exeter and Thelma Stickney of Hampton Beach.

Bill Elliot was emcee and Chuck Hill's Hampton Beach band provided the musical entertainment. Judges were John Dineen, Rolly Rogers of the Rogers Model Agency in Boston, Bill Collins of the Lawrence Sun newspaper, and models Jane Foss and Lea Jahms.

1950 Miss Hampton Beach Sally Atkinson.

Sally was crowned at the beach bandstand on the opening day of Carnival Week, August 24, 1950, with Chuck Hill's band providing the musical entertainment. Also named Queen of the Hampton Beach Carnival, she presided over the week's festivities.

Sally Atkinson walks to her crowning at the beach bandstand, August 24, 1950.

1950

1951—SONJA-BUNTY ROMER, MONTREAL QB

1951 Miss Hampton Beach Sonja-Bunty Romer at the 1952 coronation of Gaynor Jenkins.

At the pageant held on August 23, 1951, twenty-six young women vied for the title of Miss Hampton Beach. From that field, judges chose Sonja-Bunty Romer of Montreal, Quebec, described as a "tall, shapely brunette" with body measurements of "38-25-37." Second place went to model Doris Findley of Dorchester, Massachusetts, with third place going to last year's second place winner, Betty Marshall of Brookline, Massachusetts.

The first of only two Canadian women to win the title, Sonja-Bunty received $35 in cash, plus clothing, jewelry, perfume, accessories, and candy from beach businesses like the Casino Gift Shop, Dudley's Gift Shop, Lobster Pot Restaurant, the Casino-Olympia Theatres, and the Ashworth Hotel.

Bill Elliot was emcee and Chuck Hill's Hampton Beach band provided musical entertainment for the pageant. Judges were beach business owners John Dineen, Joseph Flynn, Henry Hamel, Patsy Fuller, and John Dignon. In a tradition now separated from the queen contest, the Chamber of Commerce raffled off a red Pontiac sedan, won by Mary Forte of Haverhill, Massachusetts.

In a nostalgic nod to the era of the Carnival Queens, this year's winner was allowed to choose a King to preside with her over the Carnival Week festivities. Sonja-Bunty tapped Frank Malaham of Boston, and on August 24 the pair was transported to their coronation at the bandstand on a Chamber of Commerce parade float. Outgoing queen Sally Atkinson rode on the Casino's float and placed the crown on the head of her successor. The new queen and her king presided over the inaugural Grand Carnival Ball, held at the Casino Ballroom on August 29, 1951.

1952

1952—GAYNOR JENKINS, MONTREAL QB

This year's win by Gaynor Jenkins of Montreal, Canada marked the second year in a row that a Canadian had taken the coveted crown. At the pageant held on August 21, 1952, some in the crowd of 15,000 were unhappy with the judges' choice, claiming she had been chosen only to promote tourism from Canada. In an embarrassing spectacle, they made their dissatisfaction loudly known, "vociferously" protesting the decision "over a blonde local favorite [Beverly Brindamour] and a dimpled Massachusetts brunette [Doris Dionne]," causing the teary-eyed winner to apologize "for not being as popular as I should be."

Doris Dionne of Methuen, Massachusetts was the second place winner, with "sweetly slender" Beverly Brindamour of Hampton coming in third. The unpopular judges were an unnamed "panel of harried newspapermen."

The 1952 Miss Hampton Beach court. L-r back row: third place Beverly Brindamour, Miss Shine, Claire Henneka, unknown, Miss Shine, second place Doris Dionne. L-r front row: 1950 Miss Hampton Beach Sally Atkinson, 1952 Miss Hampton Beach Gaynor Jenkins, 1951 Miss Hampton Beach Sonja-Bunty Romer (Carnival Ball, Casino Ballroom, August 27, 1952).

Carole Wheeler (Walles) of Hampton Beach competed in the 1952-1954 Miss Hampton Beach contests.

Local girl Carole Wheeler, whose family owned Dudley's Gift Shop at the beach, hailed from a long line of beach queens. Her grandmother Clara Dudley, aunt Mildred Dudley (Autio), and mother Dorothy Dudley (Wheeler) had all been Carnival Queens in their day. Carole continued the tradition by competing in the 1952, 1953, and 1954 Miss Hampton Beach pageants. In a contest held in Boston in 1953, she won the title of Miss Saleslady of the Year.

1953—JOAN AHEARN, NORTH CHELMSFORD MA

On August 27, 1953, the Miss Hampton Beach contest, with Bill Elliot in his role as master of ceremonies, was the opening feature of this year's Carnival Week. An estimated 5,000 spectators were on hand to watch the panel of judges, which included New Hampshire Governor Hugh Gregg, choose as winner 17-year-old Joan Ahearn of North Chelmsford, Massachusetts. Second place went to Joan Manning of Springfield, Massachusetts, and third place went to Peggy Castles of Medford, Massachusetts.

A parade and coronation were held the following night, and the Grand Carnival Ball was staged in the Casino Ballroom a week later, on September 2, 1953. The winning girls appeared as models at a style show at the beach, which was emceed by Bill Elliot.

1953

1953 Miss Hampton Beach Joan Ahearn and her attendants.

1953 Grand Carnival Ball (renamed Coronation Ball in 1956) with Miss Hampton Beach Joan Ahearn of North Chelmsford MA, her court, and the Ted Herbert Orchestra in the Casino Ballroom, September 2, 1953.

1954—PRISCILLA MCNALLY, HAVERHILL MA

With flooding, toppling trees, and winds gusting up to 125 mph, Hurricane Carol put a damper on this year's Carnival Week festivities. Authorities evacuated the beach, with some 2,000 people sheltering at local schools to wait out the storm.

On September 2, despite chill ocean winds that buffeted the beach after the hurricane's passing, the Miss Hampton Beach contest and crowning took place (only the Grand Carnival Ball was canceled). A "full slate" of twenty-one contestants paraded on the bandstand, with Haverhill, Massachusetts dancing instructor Priscilla McNally, "clearly the spectators' favorite," winning the title. Second place went to 17-year-old Barbara Ann Curran of Waltham, Massachusetts, with Beverly Brindamour of Hampton taking third. New Hampshire Governor Hugh Gregg and the outgoing queen Joan Ahearn (Junkins) presented the awards.

The Hurricane Queen. Coronation of 1954 Miss Hampton Beach Priscilla McNally and King Jack Berry (hometown unknown) at the Hampton Beach bandstand, September 2, 1954.

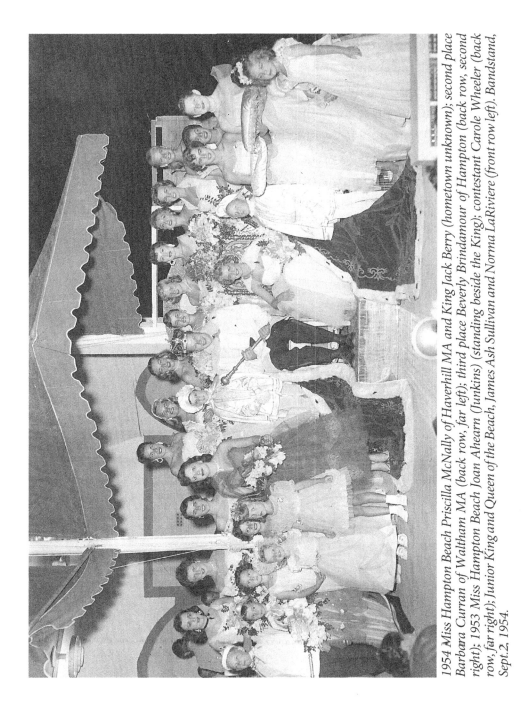

1954 Miss Hampton Beach Priscilla McNally of Haverhill MA and King Jack Berry (hometown unknown); second place Barbara Curran of Waltham MA (back row, far left); third place Beverly Brindamour of Hampton (back row, second right); 1953 Miss Hampton Beach Joan Ahearn (Junkins) (standing beside the King); contestant Carole Wheeler (back row, far right); Junior King and Queen of the Beach, James Ash Sullivan and Norma LaRiviere (front row left). Bandstand, Sept.2, 1954.

1955—BARBARA ANN CURRAN, WALTHAM MA

1955

The usual order of the Miss Hampton Beach pageant and ball was changed this year to allow spectators a pre-pageant look at the 24 contestants. To that end, the Grand Carnival Ball was held a week before the September 1, 1955 contest. The queen's coronation went on as usual the day after the contest. Judges chose as winner last year's first runner up, Barbara Ann Curran of Waltham, Massachusetts. For her win she received $200 cash and other gifts. Second place went to Sandra Sadowsky of Kittery, Maine, who weeks before had won the title of Miss Sea Nymph (*see page 66*). Judy Anderson of Woburn, Massachusetts, the winner of the 1955 Miss Mermaid contest, placed third.

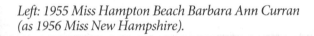

Left: 1955 Miss Hampton Beach Barbara Ann Curran (as 1956 Miss New Hampshire).

Below: 1955 Miss Hampton Beach Barbara Ann Curran on the bandstand with her court, Sept. 1, 1955.

1956—CYNTHIA FULLER, BRIGHTON MA

With advice from Alfred Patricelli of Bridgeport, Connecticut, the New England director of the Miss Universe pageant, the Hampton Chamber of Commerce made four changes to the pageant this year.

1) Traditionally held around Labor Day, the pageant was moved up to late July-early August, "to let the queen reign throughout the entire August Festival."

2) The crowning was combined with the coronation ball at the end of the month.

3) The winner-by-applause system of judging was replaced with a point system, with official tellers tallying the judges' scores.

4) Contestants were now required to be between the ages of 16-24 and never married.

1956 Miss Hampton Beach Cynthia Fuller crowned by Miss NH Barbara Ann Curran, Casino Ballroom, August 30, 1956.

At the pageant held on August 2, 1956, forty-four young women competed for the title of Miss Hampton Beach. From that field, judges chose as winner Cynthia

L-r: Cynthia Fuller, Lyla Moran, Sally Ann Freedman.

Fuller of Brighton, Mass. Second place went to Lyla Moran, 17, of Boston, and third place to Sally Ann Freedman, 16, of Peabody, Mass. Judges were Patricelli, Walter Greene of AP-Boston, David Wurzel of UP-Boston, and a Hampton Playhouse actor, Alex Reed.

1956

1956 Coronation Ball, Casino Ballroom, August 30, 1956. Back row, l-r: first runner up Lyla Moran, 1956 Miss Hampton Beach Cynthia Fuller, second runner up Sally Ann Freedman, 1956 Miss New Hampshire Barbara Ann Curran.

MISS NEW HAMPSHIRE FOR MISS UNIVERSE & MISS NEW ENGLAND BEAUTY PAGEANTS

The first Miss New Hampshire for Miss Universe contest* was held at Hampton Beach on August 23, 1956, under the direction of Miss Universe Regional Director Alfred Patricelli. Contestants could be single or married, between the ages of 18 and 28, and must be of good character.

From 1957 to 1965, the Miss New England pageant—"a beauty contest which has not been attempted before in New England"—was held in the "cool and handsome" Casino Ballroom. Many of the same girls competed in both contests, as well as in Miss Hampton Beach. The new Miss New Hampshire or Miss New England was often given the honor of crowning the new Miss Hampton Beach.

Although Barbara Ann Curran of Waltham, Massachusetts won that first pageant, the Miss New Hampshire USA website lists second place Lyla Moran of Boston, Massachusetts as the titleholder who competed in the Miss USA pageant that year.

1956 Miss New Hampshire for Miss Universe winners, l-r: second runner up Constance Ramsey, 21, Haverhill MA; winner and 1955 Miss Hampton Beach Barbara Ann Curran, 19, Waltham MA; first runner up Lyla Moran, 17, Boston MA. Casino Ballroom, August 23, 1956.

1957 Miss New England Maureen Burke, 16, of Methuen MA. She also won second place in the 1957 Miss Hampton Beach pageant.

 Regalia—In 1956 cross-body sashes made their first appearance on the Hampton Beach pageant scene.

THE WEEKLY BEAUTY CONTESTS

From 1954 to 1956, weekly beauty contests, named *Miss Personality, Miss Glamour, Miss Sunshine, Miss Sea Nymph, Miss Mermaid,* and *Miss August Festival,* were held at the Hampton Beach bandstand on Thursday nights during the month of August. Contestants were required to be 16 years of age or older, never married, nor professional models. Winners were chosen by the timing of audience applause. Rules stated that Miss Personality contestants must wear cotton dresses; Miss Glamour Girl, an evening or cocktail gown; Miss Sunshine, shorts and blouse; and Miss Sea Nymph, any beach outfit. First prize was a $100 bond. Each week's top three winners were automatically entered in the Miss Hampton Beach contest.

1954 Miss Personality winners, l-r: second place Beverly Brindamour of Hampton, winner Pat Kilbane of Dorchester MA, and third place Peg Kenney of Northampton MA. August 5, 1954.

1954 Miss Personality Pat Kilbane.

1954 Miss Personality contest at the Hampton Beach bandstand, August 5, 1954. The winner Pat Kilbane is #14.

1954 Miss Sea Nymph winners, l-r: first runner up Priscilla McNally, Haverhill MA; winner Beverly Brindamour, Hampton; second runner up Pat Melanson, Newton MA. Bandstand, August 26, 1954.

1954 Miss Sunshine winners, l-r: first runner up Priscilla McNally, Haverhill MA; winner Marion Jean Kennedy, West Swanzey NH; second runner up Bernice Brocklehurst, Montreal QB. Bandstand, August 19, 1954.

1955 Miss August Festival winner Colleen Whitely, Haverhill MA with bandleader Ray Anthony and first runner up Sandra Sadowsky, Kittery ME (far left). At the microphone is emcee Bill Elliot. Bandstand, August 4, 1955.

1955 Miss Sea Nymph Sandra Sadowsky, 18, Kittery ME (center); first runner up Lorraine St. Onge, 16, Lowell MA (winner's right); second runner up Carol Ann Mately, 19, Lowell MA (winner's left), third runner up Sally Bradshaw, Hampton (second from right). Rain sent the contest indoors. On stage is Bob Bachelder's orchestra. Casino Ballroom, August 11, 1955.

1956 Miss Sea Nymph, l-r: second runner up Judy Anderson, 18, Milford CT; winner Sally Ann Freedman, 16, Peabody MA; first runner up Marlane Decouteau, 19, Haverhill MA. Bandstand, August 9, 1956.

1956 Miss Mermaid, l-r: second runner up Lyla Moran, 17, Boston MA; winner Marlane Decouteau, 19, Haverhill MA; first runner up Sonya Rae Minks, 20, Chester NH. Bandstand, August 16, 1956.

1957

1957—SALLY ANN FREEDMAN, PEABODY MA

At the pageant held on August 7, 1957, thirty-two young women vied for the title of Miss Hampton Beach. From that field, judges chose as winner 17-year-old Sally Ann Freedman of Peabody, Massachusetts. At 16 she won Miss Sea Nymph and was second runner up in the Miss Hampton Beach pageant. In 1957 she won Miss Massachusetts, and in 1958 she won Miss Boat-O-Rama at Hampton Beach.

Second place went to Maureen Burke, 16, of Methuen, Massachusetts, who also won the title of Miss New England this year. Taking third was 17-year-old Diane Mae Wallace of Peabody, Massachusetts, who placed third in the Miss New England pageant.

Sally was crowned at the Coronation Ball held at the Casino Ballroom on August 28, 1957.

1957 Miss Hampton Beach contest, bandstand, August 7, 1957. Winner Sally Ann Freedman, 7th from left. First runner up Maureen Burke, 10th from right. Second runner up Diane Mae Wallace, 15th from left.

Above: 1957 Miss New England Maureen Burke crowns 1957 Miss Hampton Beach Sally Ann Freedman at the Casino Ballroom, August 28, 1957.

Right (l-r): First runner up Maureen Burke, 1957 Miss Hampton Beach Sally Ann Freedman, and second runner up Diane Mae Wallace. Bandstand, August 7, 1957.

1958

1958—CAROLYN ANN KOMANT, KITTERY ME

On July 29, 1958, thirty-eight young women competed for the title of Miss Hampton Beach in this final Bandstand Years contest. From that field, judges chose as winner 17-year-old Traip Academy student Carolyn Ann Komant of Kittery, Maine. For her win she received a $100 savings bond and a trophy that was presented to her by Wes Covington, leader of the Tommy Dorsey band. But for Carolyn, whose body measurements were reported to be "35-23-35," the bigger prizes, especially after she placed among the top ten finalists in the Miss USA contest the following year, were the modeling and screenacting opportunities that came her way. She went on to a brief career in both fields, with a small role in the b-movie *House of Women* (1961), appearances in ads, and roles on several TV shows, including *77 Sunset Strip*, before retiring.

1958 Miss Hampton Beach Carolyn Ann Komant at the bandstand, July 29, 1958. On her left is 1957 Miss Hampton Beach Sally Ann Freedman.

Tied for second place was 17-year-old Marie Mungovan of Belmont, Massachusetts, sponsored by the Rice Lodge, and Sandra Murrow of Salem, Massachusetts, sponsored by the Casino Penny Arcade.

Bill Elliot and Henry Hamel were the masters of ceremonies and Eddie Madden's Hampton Beach band provided the musical entertainment. The judges were AP photo editor Walter Greene of Boston; Miss Portsmouth-Miss Jubilee director Norman Landrey; WBZ-TV news editor Denny Whitmarsh; NH Planning and Development Commission director George Hagopian; and Miss Universe pageant regional director Alfred Patricelli.

Carolyn Ann Komant and attendants aboard the Miss Hampton Beach parade float on Ocean Boulevard (1958).

Coronation of 1958 Miss Hampton Beach Carolyn Ann Komant with 1958 Miss New England Doree McNamee of Brattleboro VT (left) and 1957 Miss Hampton Beach Sally Ann Freedman of Peabody MA (right). Casino Ballroom August 27, 1958.

The Grand March at the 1958 Coronation Ball, Casino Ballroom, August 27, 1958. Ladies l-r: unknown, 1957 Miss Hampton Beach Sally Ann Freedman, 1958 Miss New England Doree McNamee, 1958 Miss Hampton Beach Carolyn Ann Komant. The names of their escorts were rarely, if ever, published.

Grand March at the Coronation Ball,
Casino Ballroom, August 26, 1959.

MISS HAMPTON BEACH: THE BALLROOM ERA
1959-1976

Grand March at the Coronation Ball,
Casino Ballroom, August 24, 1962.

1959

1959—DIANE LIPSON, CRANSTON RI

In 1959 the Hampton Beach Chamber of Commerce voted to move the pageant from its breezy bandstand location indoors to the Casino* Ballroom, and in doing so launched Miss Hampton Beach into a new and exciting era of glitz and glamour. The move allowed the Chamber to charge admission to the event, and weather worries became a thing of the past. Perhaps more importantly, as Hampton Beach Casino owner John Dineen remarked at the time, the move would bring the pageant more closely in line with leading beauty contests like Miss America.

Ted Herbert's orchestra provided the musical ambiance for the 35 contestants who paraded across the stage at the inaugural indoors event, held on July 28, 1959. From this field judges chose as winner the young lady wearing the "glistening silver bathing suit and matching high heels"—17-year-old Diane Lipson of Cranston, Rhode Island. In keeping with the vogue, newspapers alerted their readers to the particulars of her "vital statistics": five-foot-six inches tall and "36-23-36."

Diane's coronation ball was held a month later. In the interim she won Miss New England Ballroom at the Surf Ballroom in Nantasket, Massachusetts. At the August 26, 1959 ball, the recently crowned Miss New England, Doree McNamee of Brattleboro, Vermont, presented the crown and title sash to Diane. John Dineen of the Casino presented her with a "giant-size" trophy and a $100 savings bond.

Marcia Zapaswick, 19, of Somerset, Massachusetts took second place, and Debbie Zabriskie, 17, of Newburyport, Massachusetts took third. Both girls were awarded a $50 savings bond.

The Casino was not (and is not) a gaming establishment. The name derives from the Italian word meaning "little house" or "country house." It was built in 1899 by the Exeter, Hampton & Amesbury Street Railway Company to encourage ridership on its line.

The Miss Hampton Beach pageant held for the first time in the Hampton Beach Casino Ballroom, July 28, 1959. The winner Diane Lipson is 7th from left.

Top left: 1959 Miss Hampton Beach Diane Lipson smiles for the camera. Top right: Diane poses with Casino owner John Dineen (right). Bottom left: West Point Cadet Fred Rice of Hampton escorts Miss Hampton Beach in the Coronation Ball Grand March, Casino Ballroom, August 26, 1959. Bottom right: West Point Cadet Fred Rice and Diane Lipson pose for the camera in the Casino Ballroom.

The 3rd Annual Miss New England pageant was held in the Casino Ballroom, August 19, 1959, with emcee Bill Elliot and Ted Herbert's orchestra. Like Miss Hampton Beach, this was a ticketed event. Marjory Jane MacLeod of Concord, New Hampshire was the winner, Joan Cole of Hull MA took second place, and Debbie Zabriskie of Newburyport MA was third.

Above left: 1959 Miss Hampton Beach Diane Lipson (left) and 1959 Miss New England Marjory Jane MacLeod. Casino Ballroom, August 26, 1959.

Above right: Marjory MacLeod received this two-foot-high trophy and the "sparkling crown" at left. The Miss Hampton Beach crown is on the right.

Left: 1959 Miss New England Marjory Jane Macleod with escort at the Coronation Ball, Casino Ballroom, August 26, 1959.

The 1959 Miss Hampton Beach court at the Coronation Ball, Casino Ballroom, August 26, 1959. 1958 Miss Hampton Beach Sally Ann Freedman (back row, left); 1959 Miss Hampton Beach Diane Lipson (back row, 4th from left); 1959 Miss New England Marjory Jane Macleod (back row, 5th from left).

1960

1960—DIANE LAUREL JESAK, DRACUT MA

On July 26, 1960, fifteen hundred people jammed the Casino to watch 36 young women vie for the title of Miss Hampton Beach. From that field of contestants, judges chose as winner 17-year-old Diane Laurel Jezak of Dracut, Massachusetts. They awarded second place to Sandie Kay, 16, of Plaistow, New Hampshire and third place to Lorraine Bourgeois, 19, of Manchester, New Hampshire.

Diane, who was a teacher at a Lowell, Massachusetts dancing academy, was crowned at the Coronation Ball held at the Casino Ballroom on August 26, 1960, during what was billed as an old-fashioned Mardi Gras Carnival Week.

1960 Miss Hampton Beach Diane Jesak on stage at the Casino Ballroom, July 26, 1960, with second runner up Lorraine Bourgeois of Manchester, New Hampshire (left) and first runner up Sandie Kay of Plaistow New Hampshire, who also won Miss New England this year (right).

The Hampton Beach strip in the 1960s. The Mardi Gras festival, so prominent in the 1920s and 1930s, returned to the beach on August 20-27, 1960, with Bill Elliot as emcee for all events at the bandstand. It was reported that presidential candidate John Kennedy had been invited but was unable to attend the week-long event.

1961—SANDIE KAY, PLAISTOW NH

The early years of the Ballroom Era saw local girls stepping into the Miss Hampton Beach limelight. Southern New Hampshire girls, including two from Hampton, won five of the first seven contests. The first in that line was Sandie Kay of Plaistow, New Hampshire, who had won Miss New England in 1960. In 1962 she won Miss New Hampshire, making her eligible to compete in the Miss Universe pageant qualifier held in Miami, Florida the following year.

With the beach pageant under the direction of Henry Hamel of the Chamber of Commerce, a fourth and fifth finalist and the title of Miss Personality were added this year. Bill Elliot reprised his role as master of ceremonies.

Second place went to Sylvia Gustavson, 19, of Winchester, Massachusetts, whose sponsor was the Hampton Atlantic station; third place went to model Su-su Smith, 21, of Newton Upper Falls, Massachusetts; fourth to Margaret Harkins, 17, of Waltham, Massachusetts (sponsor Hudon's Restaurant); and fifth place went to Jonnye McLeod, 16, of Hampton, who won the award for Miss Personality.

The Miss New England pageant. Originally held over the Labor Day holiday, the pageant was moved to an earlier date in August to allow the winner to join Miss Hampton Beach at the annual beach parade, held on August 19, 1961. The winner this year was Sylvia Gustavson of Winchester, Massachusetts.

The sixteen finalists in the 1961 Miss Hampton Beach pageant, Casino Ballroom, July 24, 1961. The winner Sandie Kay is 6th from the right. Fifth place winner Jonnye McLeod of Hampton is on the far right.

Beauty queens on stage at the Casino Ballroom, l-r: 1959 Miss Hampton Beach (and 1961 Miss New Hampshire*) Diane Lipson, 1961 Miss Hampton Beach Sandie Kay, 1958 Miss Hampton Beach Carolyn Ann Komant, 1957 Miss Hampton Beach Sally Ann Freedman.

*Diane was crowned Miss New Hampshire by Guy Lombardo at the Casino Ballroom, June 24, 1961.

Miss Hampton Beach Coronation Ball, Casino Ballroom, August 25, 1961. L-r: 1961 Miss New England Sylvia Gustavson, 1961 Miss New England first runner up Louise Richardson, 1957 Miss Hampton Beach Sally Ann Freedman, 1960 Miss Hampton Beach Diane Jesak, 1961 Miss Hampton Beach Sandie Kay.

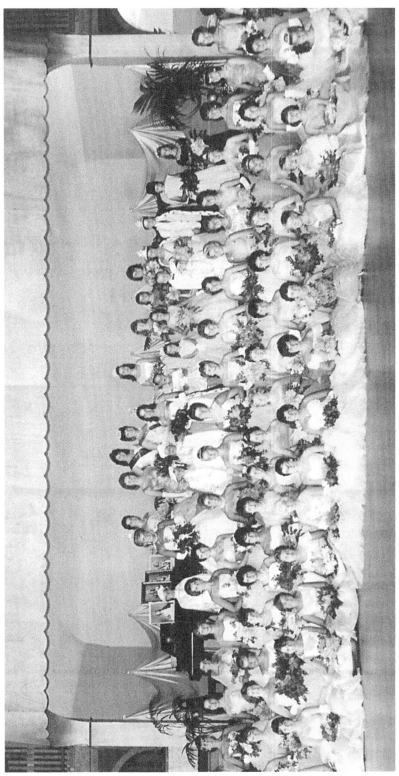

1961 Miss Hampton Beach Sandie Kay and court, Coronation Ball, Casino Ballroom, August 25, 1961.

1962 Miss New Hampshire-USA Sandie Kay, crowned at the Casino Ballroom, June 16, 1962.

Sandie was a semi-finalist in the Miss USA pageant, held in Long Beach, California on July 12, 1962. The winner of this pageant went on to compete in Miss Universe.

1962

1962—JONNYE MCLEOD, HAMPTON NH

At the pageant held on July 23, 1962, thirty-eight young women vied for the title of Miss Hampton Beach. From that field, judges chose as winner 17-year-old Winnacunnet High School graduate Jonnye McLeod, who was the first Hampton girl to win the title. Jonnye had moved from Rhode Island to Hampton with her family in 1959 when her father, a Navy officer, was assigned to the Portsmouth, New Hampshire military prison. In 1963 she attended the dedication of the new Seashell Stage at the beach, won Miss Portsmouth and Miss New Hampshire-USA, and competed but did not place in the Miss USA pageant in Miami, Florida.

Second place in the beach pageant went to Louise Richardson, 17, of Georgetown, Massachusetts, who also won Miss New England this year. Third place went to Martha Ann Wiggin, 17, of Hampton.

 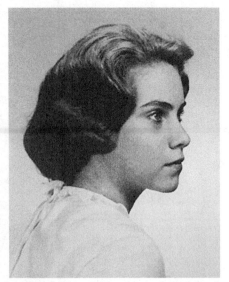

Left: Jonnye as a Winnacunnet High School cheerleader. Right: Jonnye's yearbook photograph (1962).

1962 Miss New Hampshire Sandie Kay crowns 1962 Miss Hampton Beach Jonnye McLeod, Casino Ballroom, August 24, 1962.

1962 Miss Hampton Beach Jonnye McLeod and the Junior Miss Hampton Beach (name unknown) with their parents at the Casino Ballroom, August 24, 1962.

1962 Miss Hampton Beach Jonnye McLeod and the Junior Miss Hampton Beach with Navy personnel at the Casino Ballroom, August 24, 1962.

The Grand March at the Coronation Ball, Casino Ballroom, August 24, 1962. Ladies l-r: 1957 Miss Hampton Beach Sally Ann Freedman, 1962 Miss New England Louise Richardson, 1962 Miss New Hampshire Sandie Kay, 1962 Miss Hampton Beach Jonnye McLeod (with escort Peter Moulton.)

1963

1963—BEVERLY ANN HEBERT, MANCHESTER NH

At the pageant held on July 23, 1963, thirty-seven young women vied for the title of Miss Hampton Beach. From that field, judges awarded 71 out of 100 points and the win to 18-year-old Beverly Ann Hebert of Manchester, New Hampshire, whom newspaper reports described as a 5'8" brunette with 140 "well-distributed pounds" and body measurements of "36-25-36."

Second place went to 16-year-old Winnacunnet High School student Frances Houlihan of Seabrook, New Hampshire; third to Lynda Rauding of Manchester, New Hampshire; fourth to Miss New England Louise Richardson of Georgetown, Massachusetts; and fifth place went to Nancy Joan Brackett of Brighton, Massachusetts.

Bill Elliot was the master of ceremonies, Henry Hamel the pageant director, and Frank Lawlor's Hampton Beach Concert Band provided the background music. The judges were TV personality Claire Devaney, AP photo editor Walter Greene, NE-TV newsman Denny Whitmarsh, Jack Hamilton of the Boston Globe, and Claude Higgins of the Sullivan Modeling Agency in Boston.

Beverly was crowned at the Coronation Ball held at the Casino Ballroom on August 21, 1963. The following year she won Miss New Hampshire-USA and competed without placing in the Miss USA pageant held in Miami, Florida.

"Displaying near perfect poise," Frances Houlihan of Seabrook, New Hampshire (center) won the 7th Annual Miss New England pageant, Casino Ballroom, August 13, 1963. First runner up Lynda Rauding of Manchester NH (left), second runner up Nancy Brackett of Brighton MA (right), not shown is third runner up Janice Fay of Methuen MA.

1964

1964—SHEILA SCOTT, HAMPTON BEACH NH

At the pageant held on July 21, 1964, thirty-eight young women vied for the title of Miss Hampton Beach. From that field, judges chose as winner 16-year-old Winnacunnet High School cheerleader Sheila Scott of Hampton Beach, who would be crowned at the Coronation Ball held at the Casino Ballroom on August 21, 1964.

Originally from England, Sheila emigrated with her family from Canada to the United States in 1962. As a vocalist, she led the 1964 season's senior division in the weekly beach talent shows. Her mother ran the Somerset Lodge at the beach, but, as Sheila tells it, was forced out by the 1960s-era riots that damaged her business. In 1967 Sheila won Miss New Hampshire and competed in the Miss America pageant, where she was voted Miss Congeniality. In 1968 she toured southeast Asia with the USO to entertain US troops.

Second place in the pageant went to Sheila's classmate, Frances Houlihan of Seabrook, and third place went to Frances Janes of Lynn, Massachusetts. Bill Elliot was master of ceremonies and Stan Bednarz's band played background music. The judges were Stan Selib, Miss Universe pageant director; Arnold Harklow, Ward Griffith ad agency; Frank Murphy, AP New England; Park Finlay, Record American newspaper; and John Vari, Hampton Playhouse owner.

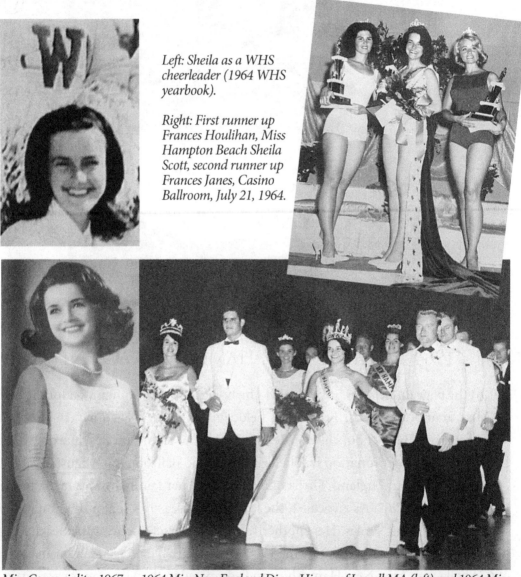

Left: Sheila as a WHS cheerleader (1964 WHS yearbook).

Right: First runner up Frances Houlihan, Miss Hampton Beach Sheila Scott, second runner up Frances Janes, Casino Ballroom, July 21, 1964.

Miss Congeniality, 1967 Miss America pageant.

1964 Miss New England Diane Higson of Lowell MA (left) and 1964 Miss Hampton Beach Sheila Scott lead the Grand March at the Coronation Ball, Casino Ballroom, August 21, 1964.

BANDLEADER STAN BEDNARZ

Stan Bednarz was Hampton's Winnacunnet High School music director from 1961 to 1999. He conducted the Hampton Beach Concert Band from 1964 until the daily bandstand concerts ended in 1984. However, Stan and his orchestra continued to provide musical entertainment at the beach for many years after.

Stan's band played the Miss Hampton Beach pageant from 1974 to 1982 (with the exception of 1977, when a band called The Lords played). After Stan's run, The Continentals took over and played the pageants until 1995.

In 1977 Bednarz played at the 50th wedding anniversary of his friends Bill and Alzena Elliot (a longtime emcee of the beauty contests, Bill is famously remembered at the "Singing Cop" of Hampton Beach). When Stan retired from teaching in 1999, the high school's music room was named in his honor.

The Stan Bednarz Band at the Seashell Stage, c. 1975.

The Sea Shell

1
9
6
5

1965—JUDY REYNOLDS, MANCHESTER NH

This year marked the fifth consecutive year that a Granite Stater had won Miss Hampton Beach. At the pageant held on July 20, 1965, thirty-seven young women vied for the title. From that field, judges chose as winner 18-year-old markswoman Judy Reynolds of Manchester, New Hampshire, awarding her 89 out of a possible 100 points. Newspaper reports described Judy, who was sponsored by the Hale Shoe Store in Hampton, as 5'6", 127 lbs, with "vital statistics" of 36-24-35. Frances Houlihan of Seabrook again took second place. Third place went to Carol Seega of Worcester, Massachusetts; fourth to Anita Finnegan of Hyde Park, Massachusetts; and fifth to Candye Walker of Paris, France.

Judy was crowned by outgoing queen Sheila Scott at the Coronation Ball held at the Casino Ballroom on August 20, 1965.

Bill Elliot was master of ceremonies and Henry Hamel was the pageant's director. Judges were Roger Harris of McCall's, WBZ Radio on-air personality Denny Whitmarsh, Miss Universe pageant director Stan Selib, Jasper Yeomans of Coca Cola, and Record American Ballroom Editor Eddie Rugg.

This year, 1965, would be the last year of the Miss New England pageant, won by Anita Finnegan of Hyde Park, Massachusetts.

Above: The final fifteen contestants in the 1965 Miss Hampton Beach pageant. Winner Judy Reynolds is 6th from left, first runner up Frances Houlihan is 3rd from right, and second runner up Carol Seega is 2nd from left. Casino Ballroom, July 20, 1965.

Right: 1965 Miss Hampton Beach winners, l-r: first runner up Frances Houlihan, queen Judy Reynolds, second runner up Carol Seega. 1964 Miss Hampton Beach Sheila Scott at right. Casino Ballroom, July 20, 1965.

Outgoing queen Sheila Scott crowns Judy Reynolds at the Coronation Ball, Casino Ballroom, August 20, 1965.

1965 Miss Hampton Beach Judy Reynolds on the beach with contestants in the 1966 pageant, July 1966.

1966

1966—MARYLEE HOULE, WORCESTER MA

In 1962 the State of New Hampshire replaced the aging beach bandstand with an outdoor entertainment complex called the Seashell. On August 5, 1966, the Miss Hampton Beach pageant was held there, before the general public, with Dana Hull of Redbook magazine as master of ceremonies and a total of 38 contestants vying for the title. With points tied for first place, the two girls with identical scores were called back onstage. After the judges rescored, 19-year-old Marylee Houle of Worcester, Massachusetts, who had been coming to Hampton Beach with her family every summer for 18 years, and who worked at Giovanni's Restaurant on the beach, was declared the winner. Catherine Hisnette, also of Worcester, took second place. Third place went to Irene Martineau of Manchester, New Hampshire; fourth to Nancy Lee Taft of Baldwinville, Massachusetts; and fifth to Lorraine Drouin of Lowell, Massachusetts. Robin Henderson was the lone entry from Hampton.

On August 16, 1966, Marylee was crowned by outgoing queen Judy Reynolds at the Seashell Stage.

1967

1967—SALLY GAINES, DURHAM NH

On July 25, 1967, five thousand spectators gathered at the open air Seashell Stage to watch 24 young women vie for the title of Miss Hampton Beach. From that field, judges chose as winner 19-year-old college student Sally Gaines, a first-time pageant contestant from Durham, New Hampshire. Newspaper reports described her as "petite and attractive, 5'3" tall and weighing 110 lbs. Her vital statistics are 34-23-34."

At the pageant hosted by WMUR-TV news director Ed Williams and 1967 Miss New Hampshire Sheila Scott, the press "unanimously voted" Sally their choice "shortly after she first appeared on stage." It was reported that she received rounds of applause from the audience whenever she appeared. Second place went to Judy

Callender, 18, of Dover, New Hampshire; third to Starr Lea Paine, 16, of Amesbury, Massachusetts; fourth to Jeanna Cavanaugh, 20, of Westfield, Massachusetts; and fifth place went to Kris Jackson, 18, of Rye, New Hampshire. Sally was crowned at the Coronation Ball held at the Casino Ballroom on August 1, 1967.

Outgoing queen Marylee Houle crowns 1967 Miss Hampton Beach Sally Gaines, Seashell Stage, July 25, 1967.

L-r: first runner up Judy Callender, 1967 Miss Hampton Beach Sally Gaines, pageant co-host 1967 Miss New Hampshire Sheila Scott, and pageant co-host WMUR-TV news director Ed Williams, Coronation Ball, Casino Ballroom, August 1, 1967.

1968

1968—GRETCHEN WOOD, WEST NEWBURY MA

After the Seashell Stage experiment of the previous two pageants, Miss Hampton Beach returned to the Casino Ballroom this year. The contest and crowning were combined into a single, one-night event, and the Coronation Ball, held since 1951, was no longer a part of the pageant.

At the pageant held on July 25, 1968, thirty young women competed for the title of Miss Hampton Beach. From that field, judges awarded first place to 17-year-old Gretchen Wood of West Newbury, Massachusetts; second place to Carol Stone of East Hampton, Connecticut; third to Eileen O'Connor of Lynnfield, Massachusetts; fourth to Cynthia Peters of Dover, New Hampshire; and fifth place to Gail Wilson of Littleton, Massachusetts.

WMUR-TV news director Ed Williams and Miss New Hampshire Sheila Scott again co-hosted the pageant. Sheila sang between competitions and the Stan Bednarz Band provided background music. The judges were Robbie Beckman, Haverhill Gazette; Betty Driscoll, Portsmouth Herald, Fred Rotman, Sullivan ad agency; WBZ Radio announcer Gary LaPierre; Arnold Harklow, Ward Griffith ad agency; Bob Bergen; Worcester Telegram; Portsmouth, New Hampshire mayor Eileen Foley.

1969—EILEEN O'CONNOR, LYNNFIELD MA

Evening gowns were added to the Miss Hampton Beach pageant so the winner would be eligible to compete in the Miss World USA contest to be held in Baltimore, Maryland later in the year. Since then, the evening gown set has been an important part of the pageant.

1969 Miss Hampton Beach Eileen O' Connor.

At the pageant held on July 24, 1969, twenty-one young women vied for the beach title. After multiple rounds of judging, the five finalists were each asked a question by the emcee, WRKO-Boston disc jockey Bobby Mitchell. With the first moon landing at the top of the nation's mind, to the question "Would you like a seat in the next space flight?," the eventual winner, Eileen O'Connor of Lynnfield, Massachusetts, said she would. (Intelligent as well as adventurous, Eileen went on to become a prosecuting attorney in Massachusetts and Florida.)

The four runners up were Wendy Lee Mitchell, April Dow, Sally Johnson, and Carolyn Perry. Judges were Betty Driscoll, Portsmouth Herald; Bob Bergen, Worcester Telegram; Arnold Harklow, Ward Griffith ad agency; Carl DeSuze, WBZ Radio; Fred Rotman, Sullivan ad agency; former Miss Massachusetts Pamela Procter;

Portsmouth, New Hampshire mayor and state senator Eileen Foley. Folk singers Terry and Don and the Claretta Dancers of Denver, Colorado entertained the audience between judging rounds.

(In another important change, guaranteed to upset some beach-goers, one-way traffic restrictions on Ocean Boulevard, lasting from mid-May until mid-September, went into effect this year.)

1970—JANICE JANES, LYNN MA

1970

Miss Hampton Beach Janice Janes.

Wearing a polka-dot bikini and unable to speak above a whisper due to a recent tonsillectomy, twenty-year-old Boston University senior Janice Janes of Lynn, Massachusetts won Miss Hampton Beach "before a crowd of hundreds" at the Casino Ballroom on July 23, 1970.

A swimsuit parade of contestants came first, with emcee Larry Justice of WBZ Radio announcing to the audience each girl's name, address, and "vital statistics." This was followed by an evening gown competition which pared the original field of 23 to 14. The swimsuit judging pared the field to ten before the five finalists were announced. Judges awarded second place to Diana Gangi of Woburn, Massachusetts; third to Dolores Vachon of South Berwick, Maine; fourth to Gail Wilson of Chestnut Hill, Massachusetts; and fifth place to Rita Wetherbee of Littleton, Massachusetts.

Robert Preston directed the pageant and the Stan Bednarz Band provided the musical entertainment. The names of the judges were not reported this year.

Regalia—The ersatz monarch's cape, worn by Miss Hampton Beach and Miss New England for many years, saw its last call to duty at Janice Janes's coronation this year.

1971—JANE FLOREN, BRADFORD MA

With no idea of winning, Haverhill High School graduate and first-time contestant Jane Floren (later known as Jan Angela Fiorentini) entered the Miss Hampton Beach pageant "on a whim." At the pageant held on July 22, 1971, she not only won the title in a field of 17 entrants, but also received a paid trip to compete that year in the Miss World USA pageant held in Hampton, Virginia, where she placed fourth. Jane went on to become a flight attendant and an artist.

Second place went to 18-year-old Pam Chaffee of Epping, New Hampshire; third to Gail Wilson, 20, of Littleton, Massachusetts; fourth to Gina Philbrick, 19, of Plymouth, New Hampshire; and fifth place to Susan Barnaby, 18, of Hampton Falls, New Hampshire.

The judges were Portsmouth mayor and state senator Eileen Foley; state official George Gilman; George Snyder of Greyhound Lines; Richard Stetson, Muscular Dystrophy Association; Sumner Friedman, Wilson, Epstein, and Freedman ad agency. The Stan Bednarz Band provided the musical entertainment.

"I've been coming to Hampton Beach ever since I was a little girl."—1971 Miss Hampton Beach Jane Floren.

 Regalia—Stemless "English monarch"-style trophies were introduced this year and lasted through the 1974 season. The sequin cape, as worn by Jane in the photo above and first seen in photos dating from 1956, remained in use through the 1988 season.

1972

1972—PEGGY ANN JACOBSON, SIMSBURY CT

Another first-time beauty pageant contestant, 18-year-old college student Peggy Ann Jacobson of Simsbury, Connecticut was working as a waitress at the Ashworth Hotel on Hampton Beach when her mother saw the Miss Hampton Beach entry form in the Beachcomber summer weekly and suggested that she enter the contest, to be held at the Casino Ballroom on July 24, 1972. The local newspaper ran an article with bios and photos of Peggy and eleven other contestants to promote the pageant, touting it as "the most fascinating on the east coast."

With "an aura of excitement and anticipation hover[ing] over the beach," an estimated 700 spectators turned out to see Peggy, described as a "stately beauty," win the title in a field of 24 contestants. She received a $125 cash prize and "the opportunity for paid radio and television representing Hampton Beach."

Last year's second place winner, Pam Chaffee of Epping, New Hampshire, again took second place; Diane Levesque, 19, also from Epping, took third; Diane McIsaac, 21, of Boston, Massachusetts was fourth; and June Tedeschi, 19, of Exeter, New Hampshire took fifth place.

Larry Justice of WBZ Radio was the master of ceremonies and the Stan Bednarz Band provided the musical entertainment for the event, at which the Chamber of Commerce presented Casino owner John Dineen with a plaque in recognition of his many years of service to the pageant.

1972 Miss Hampton Beach Peggy Ann Jacobson.

1973

1973—PAM CHAFFEE, EPPING NH

Before winning Miss Hampton Beach at the pageant held on July 23, 1973, Pam Chaffee won Miss Epping in 1969, Miss Coast Guard in 1971, and Miss Stratham Fair and Miss Granite State Vacationer in 1972. She had competed in Miss Hampton Beach three times, with two previous second place finishes. This year her mother warned her not to cut her hair before the pageant, but the hairstyle change did not keep the Plymouth State College business major from winning the title in a field of 33 contestants. For her win, Pam was awarded a $125 cash prize and the chance to work for WMUR-TV in Manchester, New Hampshire.

Taking second place was 23-year-old Linda Dylingowski, a magician's assistant from Danvers, Massachusetts. Twenty-year-old Sheila Harrington of West Roxbury, Massachusetts was third; Caron Elizabeth Coyne of Farmington, Maine, fourth; and Laura Ellen Hegerty of Sudbury, Massachusetts, took fifth place.

WBZ Radio on-air personality Larry Justice emceed the pageant, which was attended by an estimated 800 spectators. Judges were Boston Bruins player Don Awrey, New Hampshire state senator Robert Preston, Rockingham County attorney Carleton Eldridge, WMUR-TV news director Fred Kocher, Hampton Union editor Melody Dahl, and Mrs. Lilith McLoughlin.

1973 Miss Hampton Beach Pam Chaffee.

1974

1974—TEMPLE BRUNER, GROTON MA

At the pageant held on July 22, 1974, thirty-three young women vied for the title of Miss Hampton Beach. From that field, judges chose as winner 21-year-old Temple Bruner of Groton, Massachusetts. Newspaper reports described the Burlington, Massachusetts mall employee as a "five foot four-and-a-half-inch brunette…whose attractive figure measures 35-24-34." Temple won a cash prize of $150 and "the opportunity to represent the Hampton Beach area on radio and television."

Gail Marie Bissonette of Lawrence, Massachusetts took second place and Michele Corbell of Bradford, Massachusetts was third. The names of the fourth and fifth place winners were not reported. WBZ Radio on-air personality Larry Justice was the pageant emcee and the Stan Bednarz Band provided the background music.

The judges were New Hampshire state representative Wilfred Cunningham, Stratham Fair Queen pageant coordinator "Mike" Grannon, Advertising VP Dan McDougall, Miss Coast Guard pageant director Vivian Kane, and Continental Trailways manager J.J. Routhier.

1974 Miss Hampton Beach evening gown competition. Casino Ballroom, July 22, 1974.

1974 Miss Hampton Beach pageant judges, l-r: Wilfred Cunningham, "Mike" Grannan, Daniel McDougall, Vivian Kane, J.J. Routhier. Casino Ballroom, July 22, 1974.

In 1974 the pageant honored 76-year-old Blanche Thompson, who still spent her summers at Hampton Beach and still wore the diamond ring she received for winning the 1915 Queen of the Carnival contest. Blanche is shown here with Miss Hampton Beach, Temple Bruner of Groton MA. Casino Ballroom, July 22, 1974.

1973 Miss Hampton Beach Pam Chaffee (left) and 1974 Miss Hampton Beach Temple Bruner. Casino Ballroom, July 22, 1974.

1
9
7
5

1975—MARA JOAN ZWEMKE, GREENFIELD MA

In 1975 the Chamber of Commerce received a letter from the National Organization of Women, urging it to discontinue beauty pageants. "Such competitions in which women and young children vie for honors based on physical attributes are demeaning to women," wrote Anita Durel, the president of the local NOW chapter. The annual Miss Hampton Beach contest went on as usual, but after a decade of activism the movement had achieved a minor victory: by the mid-1980s the public no longer considered it acceptable for pageant hosts or the press to comment on the contestants' body measurements and the practice was ended.

1975 Miss Hampton Beach Mara Joan Zwemke.

It was a "record-breaking crowd" that filled the Casino Ballroom on July 21, 1975 to watch twenty-five young women vie for the title of Miss Hampton Beach. From that field, judges chose as winner 19-year-old Mara Joan Zwemke of Greenfield, Massachusetts, a 1974 graduate of Stoneleigh-Burnham School for Girls, whose sponsor was the Hampton Beach Casino Supper Club.

Newspaper reports described Mara as "5 feet, 9 inches tall and weighs 119 pounds. Her measurements are 36-24-36." She was awarded a trophy and a $150 cash prize.

Second place went to Betty Ann Ciolek of Peabody, Massachusetts. Third place went to Noreen Ann Brogan of Reading Massachusetts, the reigning Miss Coast Guard of Newburyport, Massachusetts. Mary Brucato of North Andover and Peggy Spellacy of Hampton rounded out the list of five finalists.

Bob Raleigh of WHDH Radio-Boston was the pageant host and the Stan Bednarz Band played background music. The judges were Carol Nashe and Arlene Heimlich, Boston Modeling Agency; photographer Robert C. Jeeves, Portsmouth, New Hampshire; entertainers Diane and George Duval of Lawrence, Massachusetts.

Regalia—The towering tiara that had dominated winners' heads since 1957 was replaced this year by a smaller crown better suited to the more relaxed styles of the 1970s. The squat "English-monarch"-style trophy, introduced in 1971, was given a long stem this year.

1976

1976—DEBRA MAURICE, SPRINGFIELD MA

The queen's cash prize was increased to $500 this year, with $100 for second place and $50 for third. Earlier in the year, Debra Maurice had won the Miss American Beauty pageant in her hometown of Springfield, Massachusetts, for which she had been awarded a trip to Bermuda. She said that a need for spending money on the trip prompted her to go for the newly-fattened Hampton Beach contest purse. That need was fulfilled when, on July 19, 1976, with ventriloquist Gary Brodeur hosting the pageant before a crowd of 1,000 spectators in the Casino Ballroom, Debra outdid 43 other contestants to win the beach title.

Miss Hampton Beach:
The Club Casino Era
1977-1996

Hampton Beach Casino owner Fred Shaake, c. 1976.

In the fall of 1976 a group of local businessmen bought and renovated the Casino complex. Led led by Hampton Beach entrepreneur Fred Shaake, who once worked at the Casino as a teenager, they redecorated the Ballroom and renamed it Club Casino (although the name appears to have been last used in 1990, for simplicity we have retained it to the end of this pageant era). Initially the club operated lounge style, with no concerts or rock and roll. Nightly acts that played popular music of the 40s, 50s, and modern disco replaced the big bands of the Ballroom era.

The popularity of the Miss Hampton Beach pageant continued to soar. Often more than a thousand spectators were in attendance, and tickets that sold for $2.50 in 1976 had risen to $10 by the early 1990s. The number of contestants averaged 33 per year, but in 1978 a ticketed audience and contestant record was set when 1,400 people were on hand to watch 61 contestants vie for the title.

In 1985 and 1986, Miss Hampton Beach was an official qualifying pageant for the Miss New Hampshire Scholarship, whose winner competed in the Miss America pageant. Because of this affiliation contestants were required to perform a two-minute talent routine, which counted for 50% of their final score. The talent competition was eliminated in 1987 when Miss Hampton Beach affiliated with Miss USA.

In 1990 the Chamber of Commerce canceled the pageant, citing scheduling and financial problems. The pageant was restarted the following year, but in the interim the reigning Miss Hampton Beach, Sabrina Dennison, agreed to keep her title for another year. She was the first of two beach queens to hold a two-year reign—the second was Stephanie Lussier of Manchester, New Hampshire, who was crowned by 90-year-old beach icon Bill Elliott at the fiftieth anniversary pageant in 1995.

The contest was again canceled in 1996. Although disputed by some, the official reason given was a lack of contestants. As it turned out, 1995 was the last year of Miss Hampton Beach at the Club Casino/Ballroom.

The Hampton Beach Casino in the 1970s.

1
9
7
7

1977—TARA DONNELLY, NORTH ANDOVER MA

At the pageant held on July 19, 1977, "the largest crowd ever" attended the Club Casino to watch thirty-two young women vie for the title of Miss Hampton Beach. From that field, judges chose as winner 16-year-old high school junior Tara Donnelly of North Andover, Massachusetts, who was awarded the top prize of $500. Second place and $100 went to 17-year-old high school senior Hollis Colby of Lynnfield, Massachusetts; third place and $50 went to 21-year-old nursing student Barbara Jo Kelly of Malden, Massachusetts.

After the swimsuit and evening gown competitions, emcee Duncan Dewer of WHEB Radio posed poise questions to the five finalists. To the lighthearted question,

"What do you look for in a boyfriend?," Tara said that he must "be very friendly, have a good personality, be very loyal, very good looking, and be all mine."

A group called The Lords provided the music for the pageant. The judges were Robin Haines, Modeling Techniques; George Hamilton, New Hampshire Parks and Recreation; Richard Christofore, Greyhound Lines; Ron Allard, WKXR Radio; 1966 Miss Hampton Beach Marylee Houle.

1977 Miss Hampton Beach Tara Donnelly.

1
9
7
8

1978—KIM FONTAINE, WORCESTER MA

The July 17, 1978 pageant set a ticketed audience and entrant record, with 1,400 spectators on hand to watch 61 young women vie for the title of Miss Hampton Beach. From that field, judges chose as winner 21-year-old college student Kim Fontaine of Worcester, Massachusetts, a frequent beauty contest participant who had won the Worcester Oktoberfest and Miss Gloria Stevens pageants in 1976. Reflecting that she failed to place in the 1975-1976 Miss Hampton Beach pageants, she said it was the most difficult pageant "because of the number of contestants." She won a trophy and a $500 cash prize.

Emcee for the pageant was Donn Tibbetts of the Manchester Union Leader newspaper. To his question, "What do you feel is the most serious problem facing our country?," Kim answered, "America's a great country, but there's a lack of feeling and respect for one another."

Second place and $100 went to Renee Dussault, 18, of Lowell, Massachusetts. Third place and $50 went to Carolyn Ann Marcil, 21, of Chelmsford, Massachusetts.

The judges were James Donahue, Hampton Beach lifeguards; James Driscoll, NH Office of Vacation Travel; Joanne Kapnis, McDougall Associates; 1973 Miss Hampton Beach Pam Chaffee (Vaughan); Joan Lord, Miss Coast Guard pageant.

Contestants wait their turn to appear on stage in the evening gown competition. 1978 Miss Hampton Beach pageant, Casino Ballroom, July 17, 1978.

1
9
7
9

1979—LOUISE MCDEVITT, LAKEWOOD CO

At the pageant held on July 16, 1979, fifty-eight young women competed for the title of Miss Hampton Beach. From that field, judges chose as winner 18-year-old Louise McDevitt of Lakewood, Colorado. When emcee Donn Tibbetts asked her who her favorite Red Sox player was and why, her answer was that she didn't follow baseball and didn't know the names of the players. Originally from Tewksbury, Massachusetts, Louise lived with her family in Colorado where she attended the University of Colorado. A summer employee of Giovanni's Restaurant, she said she had been coming to the beach since she was a young girl. Newspaper reports described her as weighing 116 lbs, with "vital statistics" of 34-25-33. She took away a trophy and a $500 cash prize.

Second place and $100 went to Diane McGarry, 18, of Manchester, New Hampshire. Third place and $50 went to Patricia Kavanaugh, 18, of Westford, Massachusetts. A local girl, 19-year-old Linda Anne Brackett of Hampton Falls, was one of the five finalists.

Judges were Barbara Tyler, VP John Robert Powers, Boston; Fred Nash, NH Seacoast Region Association; Dr. John McGinness, sing-a-long leader at Hampton Beach; Cynthia Erb Kuehl; 1949 Miss Hampton Beach Caryle Cadario (Gleason); 1974 Miss Hampton Beach Temple Bruner.

 Regalia—The crown on the winner's trophy was all but forgotten about this year as the style reverted to a taller, more angular silhouette. This style was short-lived, lasting only through the 1981 season.

KIM FONTAINE
1978

Sponsored by:
Hampton Beach Area Chamber of Commerce

1980

1980—KATHLEEN ANN ROGERS, SEABROOK NH

On July 22, 1980, hundreds of spectators paid four dollars apiece to watch the 35th annual Miss Hampton Beach pageant, staged at the Club Casino by beach businesswomen Harriet McCurdy and Barbara Simeone. The emcee was ventriloquist Gary Brodeur—who had last hosted the pageant in 1976—and his dummy "pal" Rusty Daniels. From a field of some 40 contestants, the judges chose as winner 17-year-old Kathleen Ann Rogers of Seabrook, New Hampshire.

Kathleen worked as a maid at the Ashworth Hotel and had entered the contest at the request of the hotel's gift shop manager. Even with her prior modeling experience, during the evening gown competition all she could think of "was not to fall off my shoes."

With the title of Miss Hampton Beach, Kathleen received a trophy and a $500 cash prize. She would go on to win Miss New Hampshire-USA in 1982.

Second place and $100 cash went to Debbie Peltonovich, 22, of Atkinson, New Hampshire, who was sponsored by the Tides Motel. Third place and $50 cash went to Julie Delaney, 17, of Dayton, Ohio, sponsored by Yankee Lady. Fourth went to Sandra Fairbrother, 18, of Haverhill, Massachusetts, sponsored by Surf Side Chalet; fifth place went to Caron Leslie Caetano, 21, of Woburn, Massachusetts, sponsored by the Windsor Motel.

The judges were modeling school director Mrs. Paul Heintz, photographer Ralph Morang, Hampton dress shop owner Aurelie Amante, model and Hampton native Diana LaValle, and Patrick Lyon, owner of Boston-Boston disco.

1981—DIANE MCGARRY, MANCHESTER NH

At the pageant held on July 21,1981, about thirty young women vied for the title of Miss Hampton Beach. From that field, judges chose as winner 19-year-old Diane McGarry of Manchester, New Hampshire, who in 1980 won the titles of Miss Winnipesaukee, Miss New Hampshire, and competed but did not place in the Miss America pageant.

Second place went to last year's first runner up, Debbie Peltonovich of Newton, New Hampshire. The names of the other finalists were not reported this year.

1982

1982—DEBBIE PELTONOVICH, NEWTON NH

At the pageant held on July 20, 1982, an unreported number of young women vied for the title of Miss Hampton Beach. From that field, judges chose as winner 23-year-old accountant Debbie Peltonovich of Newton, New Hampshire, who had placed second in 1980 and 1981 before winning the crown this year. A self-avowed fan of jazz, she was described in newspaper reports as "an articulate, vivacious blond," 5'5" tall, 115 pounds, with body measurements of "34-24-34."

Responding to the vocal criticism of beauty pageants, Debbie said she did not think the events exploited women. "They are great entertainment," she said. "I have a wonderful time, win or lose, and I think the audiences have a great time, too."

Caron Leslie Caetano, a 1980 finalist, took second place. Marcia Hinkle, 18, of Hampton was third; Kim Renee Wever, 19, also of Hampton, was fourth; and Kimberly Ann Jackson, 21, of Methuen, Massachusetts took fifth place. The pageant was under the direction of Hampton Chamber of Commerce members June Bean and Joyce Pappademas.

Semi-finalists in the 1982 Miss Hampton Beach pageant held at the Club Casino, July 20, 1982. The Stan Bednarz Band played background music for the event.

The five finalists in the 1982 Miss Hampton Beach pageant. 1st runner up Caron Leslie Caetano is on left. Winner Debbie Peltonovich is 2nd right. Club Casino, July 20, 1982.

Top right: 1982 Miss Hampton Beach Debbie Peltonovich, Hampton Chamber of Commerce president Bernie Lemerise (center), and Hampton selectman Vic Lessard. 1982 Hampton Christmas parade.

Bottom right: Outgoing queen Debbie Peltonovich takes her final walk down the runway. Caron Leslie Caetano of Woburn MA (left) and Carrie Gard of Rye NH (right). Club Casino, July 18, 1983.

1983

1983—CARON LESLIE CAETANO, WOBURN MA

On July 18, 1983, "a night of glitter and pageantry, of nostalgia and beautiful women," with emcee WBBX Radio on-air personality Kit Baker, musical group The Continentals, and future mystery novelist Brendan Dubois covering the event for the Hampton Union newspaper, 1,200 people filled the Club Casino to watch 43 women compete for the title of Miss Hampton Beach. Repeating Debbie Peltonovich's path to success the year before, this was Caron Leslie Caetano's third-times-the-charm year. A hairdresser and cheerleader, named after the actress Leslie Caron, she had been a finalist in 1980 and 1982 before winning the crown this year. At 24 years old, she laughed that she was "a relic in pageantry."

Second place went to Maureen Haloran, 21, of Methuen, Massachusetts; third place to Danea Marie Varas of Kingston, New Hampshire; fourth to Carrie Gard, 17, of Rye, New Hampshire; and fifth to Karen Squires, 16, of Arlington, Massachusetts.

Hampton Chamber of Commerce members June Bean and Joyce Pappademas again directed the pageant, which was videotaped for replay on the local cable channel, reportedly for the first time. In response to the pageant committee's call for all Miss Hampton Beach winners to attend this year, five past winners and two women who were voted "Queen for a Day" in the 1920s appeared on stage during the event (*see photo, page 135*).

The judges were actor Alan Fleisic, former Miss New Hampshire Peggy Spellacy (Bean), Patriots cheerleader Kama George Tinios, WBZ Radio on-air personality Bob Raleigh, and press secretary Bill Herman.

Regalia—In place of the traditional trophies, the five finalists received an engraved silver bowl from Towle Silversmiths of Newburyport, Massachusetts. Finalists would receive these bowls for the next five years.

THE CONTINENTALS: ANOTHER HAMPTON BEACH TRADITION

The Continentals first played at Hampton Beach in 1977, in the lounge of the Ashworth Hotel. They played the venue every summer from 1977-1981, and then at the Seagate in 1982. From 1983-1995 they performed at the Miss Hampton Beach beauty pageant at Club Casino. With the exception of a few years, from 1977-2010 they played the Ashworth's New Year's Eve celebrations, and since 1984 have performed as part of the free summer concert series at the Seashell Stage. As Don McNeill of the band says, "seeing The Continentals at Hampton Beach has become a tradition of its own."

1983 Miss Hampton Beach winner Caron Leslie Caetano with 3rd runner up Carrie Gard and 2nd runner up Danea Marie Varas. Club Casino, July 18, 1983.

Stage director Barbara Simeone (left), Master of Ceremonies Kit Baker (center), 1983 Miss Hampton Beach Caron Leslie Caetano (right). Club Casino, July 18, 1983.

Swimsuit competition, 1983 Miss Hampton Beach pageant. Caron Leslie Caetano at center. Club Casino, July 18, 1983.

Seven former winners introduced at the 1983 Miss Hampton Beach pageant. Terry Roberts of Stratham, New Hampshire and Barbara Pearsons Carpenter of Newmarket, New Hampshire, were winners of the "Queen For A Day" contests held at the beach during the 1920s.

L-r: 1966 Miss Hampton Beach Marylee Houle, 1965 Miss Hampton Beach Judy Reynolds, 1964 Miss Hampton Beach Sheila Scott, 1954 Miss Hampton Beach Priscilla McNally, 1950 Miss Hampton Beach Sally Atkinson (Parent), Barbara Pearsons Carpenter, Terry Roberts. Club Casino, July 18, 1983.

1
9
8
4

1984—ADRIANA MOLINARI, HAMPTON NH

On July 23, 1984, an audience of 1,000 gave a standing ovation to the new Miss Hampton Beach, 16-year-old Winnacunnet High School student and first-time beauty contestant Adriana Molinari of Hampton. Originally from Uruguay, Adriana answered the emcee's onstage questions in a "charming South American accent," and, in a field of 34 contestants, "won over the judges with her brown hair, brown eyes, and 34-23-34 figure." She was sponsored by Old Time Photo at the beach.

Second place went to 17-year-old Lora Lee Langlais (hometown unknown); third to Heather Arthur, 19, of Amesbury, Massachusetts; fourth to Linda Anne Paradis, 21, of Newburyport, Massachusetts; and fifth place went to Cynthia Ann Tubbs, 24, of Worcester, Massachusetts. The five finalists were awarded cash prizes and engraved silver bowls from Towle Silversmiths of Newburyport, Massachusetts.

WHEB Radio on-air personality Kit Baker and pageant director Barbara Simeone hosted the pageant, The Continentals provided background music, and the Apple Jam Crew breakdancers entertained between elimination rounds. The judges were Boston Bruins player Rick Middleton, TV personality Tim White, TV newspersons Dale Vincent and Mickie Macklin, and 1964 Miss Hampton Beach Sheila Scott. The event was again videotaped and aired on the local cable channel.

In 1985 Adriani won Miss Teen New Hampshire All-American, and in the same pageant, Miss Photogenic and Miss Congeniality. In 1991 she won Miss New Hampshire USA, but was stripped of the title when a would-be blackmailer revealed that she worked as an exotic dancer. Capitalizing on the scandal, Adriana changed her named to Alex Taylor, continued to strip, and appeared in adult films and magazines. When asked by a reporter if she thought what she did for a living was an exploitation of women, she replied, "So are pageants, where you are standing up there in a swimsuit being judged by the size of your breasts." Coincidentally, 1984 was the last year of local newspaper coverage of contestants' "vital statistics" (bust, waist, hip measurements).

1984 Miss Hampton Beach pageant winners l-r: Linda Anne Paradis (3rd runner up), Heather Arthur (2nd runner up), Adriana Molinari, Lora Lee Langlais (1st runner up), Cynthia Ann Tubbs (4th runner up). Club Casino, July 23, 1984.

1
9
8
5

1985—MARYANNE MONTAGANO, DOVER NH

In 1985 the Hampton Chamber of Commerce affiliated the beach beauty contest with the Miss New Hampshire Scholarship, an official qualifier for the Miss America pageant. The required age range changed from 16-24 to 17-26, and, for the first time, contestants were required to perform a two-minute talent routine which would count for 50% of their final score. Tickets to the event were now $6.50.

After being bumped from its early August date at Club Casino in favor of the popular New Wave band The Squeeze, the contest was moved to the evening of August 18, 1985. The talent competition was held outdoors at the Seashell Stage over two nights, a few days before the main pageant.

"Under a kaleidoscope of multi-colored lights," winning the Miss Hampton Beach crown in a field of twenty young women was 19-year-old University of New Hampshire student Maryanne Montagano, who had been first runner up in the 1983 Miss New Hampshire Teen pageant. During the question and answer, Maryanne told the crowd of about 600 that she was ambitious and outgoing, with "a great sense of humor." In a demonstration of that humor, for her talent routine she performed a tap dance dressed as a lobster—a playful nod to her sponsor and employer, the Lobster Trap Restaurant at the beach.

Second place went to 20-year-old Heather Ann Arthur of Amesbury, Massachusetts. Third place went to the talent winner, baton-twirling Lisa Ann Vandercasteele, 21, of Salem, New Hampshire. Fourth place went to Gayle Lovejoy, 19, of Seabrook, New Hampshire, with fifth place and Miss Congeniality won by Teina Harley, 18, of Portsmouth, New Hampshire. The five finalists received cash prizes and engraved silver bowls from Towle Silversmiths of Newburyport, Massachusetts.

Barbara Simeone hosted the pageant and The Continentals provided musical entertainment. Judges were Deborah Stokel, Miss New Hampshire representative; A. Reid Bunker, Bank Meridian vice president; George Hardardt, Hampton Department of Public Works director; Mark Hatem, WNDS-TV50 salesman; Cindy Willis, Seacoast Florist; certified public accountant William Youngclaus.

OFFICIAL PROGRAM

40th Annual

Miss Hampton Beach Pageant

August 18, 1985

ANDRIANNA MOLINARI

Miss Hampton Beach 1984
Sponsored by
Hampton Beach Area Chamber of Commerce

1986—DARLA BETH JELLEY, MANCHESTER NH

This year's pageant, now called The Miss Hampton Beach Scholarship Pageant due to its continued affiliation with Miss New Hampshire-Miss America, was dedicated to Mary Ellen Burns of Salem, New Hampshire, a contestant who had been killed in a car accident while on her way to a pre-pageant interview at the beach.

At the pageant held on July 14, 1986, twenty young women vied for the title of Miss Hampton Beach. From that field, judges chose as winner 19-year-old Darla Beth Jelley of Manchester, New Hampshire. A cast member of *A Chorus Line* at the Palace Theatre in Manchester, for the talent competition Darla performed a gymnastics routine to the theme from *Flashdance*.

Second place in the overall competition went to Lisa Parnpichate, 19, of West Swanzey, New Hampshire. Third place went to Suzette King, who won the talent competition with her rendition of *Don't You Want Me Baby?* Michele Schmidt, 20, of Hampton placed fourth and Christine Gagne, 18, of Salem, New Hampshire placed fifth. The five finalists received cash awards and engraved silver bowls from Towle Silversmiths of Newburyport, Massachusetts.

The 1986 pageant was dedicated to Mary Ellen Burns of Salem NH, a contestant killed in a car accident.

Hosting the pageant again this year was Barbara Simeone, with pageant direction by Glen French and Michael Small and music by The Continentals. Before crowning her successor, outgoing queen Maryanne Montagano performed a dance routine. Judges were Jesse Marcoux, owner of Jesse's of Hampton, 1975 Miss New Hampshire Catherine Burnham, 1983 Miss New Hampshire Monica Rastallis, Miss New Hampshire pageant director William Haggerty, and Mary Bragg of the Hampton Chamber of Commerce.

1986 Miss Hampton Beach winners l-r: Suzette King (3rd), Lisa Parnpichate (2nd), Darla Beth Jelley, Michele Lee Schmidt (4th), Christine Gagne (5th). Club Casino, July 14, 1986.

1987—HEATHER LEE CHOLEWA, EXETER NH

Miss Hampton Beach affiliated with the Miss New Hampshire-USA franchise this year, thus ending the talent competition required under the Miss America pageant rules. The interview segment was also changed so that the contestants came from backstage one at a time to answer their onstage question. In what was to become a pageant tradition, contestants participated in an opening number with trained dancers. This year's dancers were from choreographer Kimberly Patent's dance school.

On July 13, 1987, before a crowd of 1,000 spectators, judges chose 18-year-old dental office secretary Heather Lee Cholewa as the 42nd Miss Hampton Beach from a "record number" of contestants. For her win, Heather was awarded a $1,000 scholarship to the Barbizon School of Modeling in Boston, Massachusetts.

Second place went to Stacie Palmer, 20, of Wilmington, Massachusetts; third to Sabrina Dennison, 19, of Portsmouth, New Hampshire; fourth to Anne-Marie Brunette, 23, of Manchester, New Hampshire; and fifth place went to Jodi Walsh, 18, of Methuen, Massachusetts.

Barbara Simeone was the emcee. The Continentals opened the show with a "variety of tunes" and provided musical entertainment throughout the show. The judges were beauty salon maven Elizabeth Grady, makeup artist David Nicholas, pageant producer Kim Savage, Barbizon School of Modeling president Lawrence Frank, and Elizabeth Howarth of Sebastian International.

42nd Annual

Miss Hampton Beach Beauty Pageant
July 13, 1987

DARLA BETH JELLY
Miss Hampton Beach 1986
Sponsored by
Hampton Beach Area Chamber Of Commerce

1987 Miss Hampton Beach Heather Lee Cholewa.

1
9
8
8

1988—LISA PARNPICHATE, WEST SWANZEY NH

At the pageant held on July 25, 1988, thirty-six young women vied for the title of Miss Hampton Beach. From that field, judges chose as winner Keene State College senior Lisa Parnpichate of West Swanzey, New Hampshire, "to an explosion of applause that rocked the Club Casino." Lisa had already competed in a total of 12 pageants, and had garnered second place in last year's Miss Hampton Beach contest. In 1990 she won Miss New Hampshire USA and competed but did not place in the Miss USA pageant. Originally from Thailand, Lisa's college major was Industrial Technology. "I like cars," she said when asked to explain her choice of field of study.

Second place went to Sabrina Dennison of Portsmouth, New Hampshire; third to Elizabeth Marr of Manchester, New Hampshire; fourth to Marianne Nicoi of Amesbury, Massachusetts; and fifth place went to Kendra Oxner of Danville, New Hampshire.

Regalia—Lisa Parnpichate was the last Miss Hampton Beach to wear the queen's sequin cape that had adorned the shoulders of winners for over thirty years. From 1989 on, capes were a thing of the past. The trophy styles reverted to the tall cup-and-figurine silhouette last seen at the 1982 pageant. With variations, this style has remained the standard.

1988 Miss Hampton Beach finalists, l-r: Kendra Oxner, Marianne Nicoi, Elizabeth Marr, Sabrina Dennison. Club Casino, July 25, 1988.

Left: 1988 Miss Hampton Beach Lisa Parnpichate and 1st runner up Sabrina Dennison. Right: Lisa parades on Ocean Boulevard at Hampton Beach.

1989-1990

1989-90—SABRINA DENNISON, PORTSMOUTH NH

At the pageant held on July 23, 1989, the judges' top choice from a field of 24 young women was 21-year-old Sabrina Dennison of Portsmouth, New Hampshire, the only deaf contestant to win the title. She was voted Miss Congeniality by her 23 co-contestants. A 1988 graduate of Portsmouth High School, "5'3" and 115 lbs," she attended Barbizon School of Modeling in Boston on a scholarship she won in a past year's competition. Prior to winning the beach title, she had placed third in 1987, second in 1988, was a semi-finalist in Miss New Hampshire USA, and had competed in Miss New Hampshire Venus. She went on to a modeling and acting career, starting with a role in the 1990 film *Santa Sangre*.

Second place went to Jane Prochadszka, 19, of Burlington Massachusetts; third place to Stacy Blaine, 22, of Bellingham, Massachusetts; fourth to Jodi Walsh, 20, of Haverhill, Massachusetts; and fifth place to Kendra Oxner, 19, of Danville, New Hampshire.

Pete Falcone of WERZ-FM Radio hosted the pageant, The Continentals provided the background music, and dance companies from the New Hampshire Academy of Performing Arts and Seacoast Civic Dance Company performed between elimination rounds.

The 44th Annual

Miss Hampton Beach Beauty Pageant

July 23, 1989

Lisa Pampichate
Miss Hampton Beach
1988

SPONSORED BY
Hampton Beach Area Chamber of Commerce

For The First Time In 75 Years
Miss Hampton Beach Pageant Cancelled

In 1990 the Chamber of Commerce canceled the pageant, citing scheduling and financial problems. The pageant was restarted the following year, but in the interim Sabrina agreed to reign for another year. She was the first of two beach queens to hold a two-year reign—the second was Stephanie Lussier of Manchester, who was crowned by 90 year old beach icon Bill Elliot at the fiftieth anniversary pageant in 1995.

1989-90 Miss Hampton Beach Sabrina Dennison.

1991

1991—MARIBETH BROWN, HOLLISTON MA

"This isn't just a beauty pageant. We're not just looking for a pretty girl to show up at a ribbon cutting. She really has to be a complete ambassador."—Pageant director Judy Dubois, quoted in the Hampton Union, July 26, 1991.

The pageant, held on July 29, 1991, was dedicated to the troops of Operation Desert Storm, and the 26 young women who vied for the title of Miss Hampton Beach were escorted to the stage by members of the US Armed Forces. From the field of contestants, judges chose as winner 21-year-old college student Maribeth Brown of Holliston, Massachusetts. The title, for which she won a $500 cash prize, qualified her to compete in Miss New Hampshire USA.

Second place went to Kerri Anne Ripel of Kensington, New Hampshire, third to Stacie Ring of Hampton, fourth to Tracy Bouthiette of Manchester, New Hampshire, and fifth place went to Mara Powell of Haverhill, Massachusetts.

Also competing were local area girls Jennifer DiDomenico of Hampton Falls, Nicole Cloutier of Exeter, Heidi Cambra of Hempstead, Christy Polizzo of Hampton, and Kelly Jean Johnson and Jennifer Perkins of Seabrook.

Darla Beth Jelly (1986 Miss Hampton Beach) and Jeff Paradis, WCQL-FM Radio, co-hosted the pageant. The judges were Mrs.

1991 Miss Hampton Beach Maribeth Brown and Glen French of the Hampton Chamber of Commerce. Casino Ballroom, July 29, 1991.

New Hampshire pageant coordinator Kim Savage; former beauty contestants Stacy Palmere and Peggy Spellacy Bean; Judy Harrington, Seacoast Fitness, Gerald Dignam, Raytheon; JoAnne Davidson, Sanders and McDermott law firm; Peter Morales, Lamie's Tavern; Marie Patent, Academy of Performing Arts.

1991 Miss Hampton Beach contestants at a pre-pageant appearance at the Seashell Stage.

1992—JENNIFER DIDOMENICO, HAMPTON FALLS NH

At the pageant held on July 27, 1992, the judges' top choice from a field of 24 young women was 21-year-old University of New Hampshire student Jennifer DiDomenico of Hampton Falls, New Hampshire. When emcee Jack Gosselin asked Jennifer what her college education meant for her future, she answered that sociology (her major) would help her gain more knowledge of social problems and allow her to become more involved in her community.

Second place went to Allyson Reynolds, 21, of Hampton; third to Jennifer Perkins, 19, of Seabrook, New Hampshire; fourth to Rachel Whitney, 18, of Somerville, Massachusetts; and fifth place went to Stacie Ring, 20, of Hampton.

46th Annual
Miss Hampton Beach
Beauty Pageant
July 27, 1992

Top: Contestants pose at the beach with Ms. American Woman New Hampshire. Bottom left: four finalists in the 1992 Miss Hampton Beach pageant, l-r: Jennifer Perkins, Rachel Whitney, Allyson Reynolds, Stacie Ring. Bottom right: Jennifer DiDomenico onstage in the swimsuit competition, Casino Ballroom, July 27, 1992.

Maribeth Brown
Miss Hampton Beach 1991

Sponsored by
Hampton Beach Area Chamber of Commerce

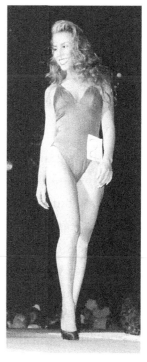

1993

1993—JULENE BRITT, WOBURN MA

At the pageant held on July 26, 1993, twenty young women vied for the title of Miss Hampton Beach. From that field, judges chose as winner 20-year-old Julene Britt of Woburn, Massachusetts, who had been among the top ten finalists in last year's pageant. A senior at Boston College, she majored in English and communications, worked as a lifeguard, volunteered at a homeless shelter, and was an intern at WCVB-TV in Boston. When emcee Jack Knox of The Continentals posed the question, "Who is the most influential person in your life and why?," Julene responded, "My Irish Catholic grandmother, who taught me to be honest and respect others and always do the best I can in whatever I choose to do with my life."

Second place and Miss Congeniality went to Stacie Ring of Hampton. The names of the other finalists were not published this year.

Glen French of the Hampton Chamber of Commerce was the pageant emcee. Pageant directors were Kim and Robyne Patent, who choreographed the dances performed by members of New Hampshire Academy of Performing Arts and Seacoast Civic Dance Company. The judges were Kim Savage, Savage Pageantry; 1989-90 Miss Hampton Beach Sabrina Dennison; Renee Shakour, Nexxus Hair Products; David Packer, Coca-Cola; Peter Morales, Lamie's Inn; and (with a fitting surname) WZEA Radio on-air personality Josh Judge.

48th Annual
Miss Hampton Beach
Beauty Pageant
July 26, 1993

Jennifer DiDomenico
Miss Hampton Beach 1992

Presented by
Hampton Beach Area Chamber of Commerce

Far left: Julene Britt onstage, swimsuit competition, Casino Ballroom, July 26, 1993.

Left: Julene Britt, emcee Glen French, and first runner up Stacie Ring, Casino Ballroom, July 26, 1993.

1993 Miss Hampton Beach finalists. Stacie Ring (left), Julene Britt (center). The names of the other finalists were not published. Casino Ballroom, July 26, 1993.

Emcee Glen French presents the Miss Congeniality Award to Stacie Ring of Hampton, Casino Ballroom, July 26, 1993.

1994

1994—LORI GREEN, BOSTON MA

At the pageant held at the Casino Ballroom on July 25, 1994, twenty-one young women competed for the title of Miss Hampton Beach. From that field, judges chose as winner 23-year-old Lori Green of Boston, Massachusetts, who had placed third in last year's Miss Massachusetts USA pageant. She was a graduate of Emmanuel College, worked at Putnam Investments, and volunteered her time with foster children. "In front of hundreds of admirers," Lori was crowned at the pageant's conclusion by outgoing queen Julene Britt.

Second place went to Stephanie Lussier, 21, of Manchester, New Hampshire; third to Kristina Michelle Hughes, 22, of Medford, Massachusetts; fourth to Mara Powell, 20, of Haverhill, Massachusetts; and fifth place went to "clear crowd favorite" Andrea Stuart, 19, of North Hampton, New Hampshire.

49th Annual
Miss Hampton Beach
Beauty Pageant
July 25, 1994

Julene Britt
Miss Hampton Beach 1993

Presented by the
Hampton Beach Area Chamber of Commerce

1994 Miss Hampton Beach Lori Green.

Admission ticket from the 1994 Miss Hampton Beach pageant.

1995-96—STEPHANIE LUSSIER, MANCHESTER NH

At the fiftieth anniversary pageant* held at the Casino Ballroom on July 31, 1995, thirty-three young women competed for the title of Miss Hampton Beach. From that field, the panel of seven judges chose as winner last year's first runner up, 22-year-old Stephanie Lussier of Manchester, New Hampshire. On hand to place the crown on her head was 90-year-old Bill Elliot, a longtime pageant emcee who was fondly recalled as the "Singing Cop" of Hampton Beach.

*Although the first named Miss Hampton Beach pageant was held in 1948, the Chamber of Commerce dated the contest's inception to 1946, when the first Miss Cover Girl contest was held. The Chamber also counted the missed pageant in 1990. By our reckoning, 1995 marked not the fiftieth, but the forty-seventh anniversary of the pageant.

At the time of her win, Stephanie was a New Hampshire College student and intern with WMUR-TV in Manchester, New Hampshire.

In her fifth and last try for the title, Stacie Ring of Hampton took second place and Miss Congeniality. Third place went to Lindsay Smith, 18, of Hampton; fourth to Christina Whicher, 16, of Houston, Texas; and fifth place went to Mara Powell, 21, of Haverhill, Massachusetts.

Five of the pageant judges were former beach queens: Priscilla McNally (1954), Debbie Peltonovich Nielson (1982), Jennifer DiDomenico (1992), Julene Britt (1993), and Sabrina Dennison (1989-90). The other judges were Kay Watkins of Ashworth by the Sea and WBZ Radio anchorman John Scott. The Continentals, Seacoast Civic Dance Company, and New Hampshire Academy of Performing Arts provided the evening's entertainment.

In 1996 the pageant was canceled. Although disputed by some, the reason given was a lack of contestants. Others cited poor management and a lack of interest in continuing the tradition. Because of the cancellation, Stephanie agreed to extend her reign for another year. Also in 1996 the first (and until 2009, the only) Little Miss and Junior Miss Hampton Beach pageant was held. Kasey Randall of Seabrook, New Hampshire won the Little Miss title and Heidi Looke of Vernon, Connecticut won the Junior Miss title. The pageant was suspended indefinitely after the murder later that year of child beauty pageant star Jon Benet Ramsay.

As it turned out, 1995 was the last year of Miss Hampton Beach at the Casino Ballroom.

Bill Elliot and 1995-96 Miss Hampton Beach Stephanie Lussier. Casino Ballroom, July 31, 1995.

MISS HAMPTON BEACH: THE SEASHELL STAGE 1997-2015

"These girls are not just beauty queens. They have drive, ambition, and they're here to win."—Miss Hampton Beach pageant director Stephanie Lussier (2005).

After the 1996 cancellation, Stephanie Lussier, the reigning Miss Hampton Beach, rescued the pageant from oblivion—and has been its enthusiastic driving force ever since. The event, she said, was a summer beach tradition that was worth saving, especially as it highlighted the positive qualities of the beach and offered young women opportunities not found elsewhere.

In July 1997 Lussier brought the pageant back to the beach, with help from the Chamber of Commerce, friends, and members of her own family (her grandmother Armande Proodian, born in 1918 and once a seamstress in a textile mill, helped out by sewing the winners' sashes, a contribution she continues to make to this day). More recently, the Hampton Beach Village District became the pageant's sponsor, and in 2016 the Hampton Historical Society began funding the queen's official photo package.

During the Ballroom/Club Casino years, Miss Hampton Beach had been a glitzy evening affair with an air of glamour and sex appeal. Under Lussier's direction the pageant focused on finding the right girl to promote Hampton Beach as a family resort destination. The contest was now a free event held on Sunday afternoon, outdoors at the Seashell Stage.

Although the pageant was now independent of the competitive circuit, contestants were still evaluated for their physical beauty, poise, and personality, and judging continued the traditional format of pre-event and onstage interviews, evening gown and swimsuit competitions. Applicants were still required to be between the ages of 16 and 24, single, never married, and without children. During her reigning year, the queen was expected to represent Hampton Beach at community events like the Easter Egg Dig, Sand Sculpting Contest, Children's Day, and the Christmas Parade.

The live bands that played the Ballroom-era pageants were replaced with recorded music. The interludes of choreographed dancing and singing remained, with the contestants performing an opening number with dancers from New England Patriot cheerleader Heidi Sullivan (Laroche)'s Dance Vision Network of Manchester, New Hampshire. The prestige (and, hence, reporting of the names) of the judges became less relevant in this period.

While the event was once again subject to the vagaries of the weather, it was never canceled or rescheduled, even when it rained or, as in 2011, when the new Seashell Pavilion was under construction, pushing the pageant onto a temporary stage on the sands in front of the Playland Arcade.

In 2009 the Little and Junior Miss Hampton Beach pageants were re-introduced. These contests, which were held on the same weekend as the adult event, brought girls as young as eight into the pageant scene, with some going on to compete in the Miss Hampton Beach contest.

The number of contestants in this period dropped from an average of thirty-three in the Ballroom years to an average of fifteen. The high was 28 in 2006; in 2015 only nine girls showed in the Miss competition. Granite State girls have dominated the pageant: of the 19 winners, 11 were from New Hampshire, 7 from Massachusetts, and 1 from Rhode Island. The lone Hampton winner was local surfer Leah Grondin, who took the title in 2007. Regardless of their hometown status, however, many of the winners had spent their childhood summers at Hampton Beach and considered it their second home.

1
9
9
7

1997—JULIE RUSSELL, WOBURN MA

At the pageant held at the Seashell Stage on July 27, 1997, twelve young women competed for the title of Miss Hampton Beach. From that field, the judges chose as winner 21-year-old Julie Russell of Woburn, Massachusetts. A contestant in the 1994 and 1995 pageants, she competed this year against her younger sister Michelle, whom she talked into entering when she found out more contestants were needed to make the pageant viable. At the time of her win, Julie was a waitress in Plymouth, Massachusetts and was completing studies in Spanish and law at the University of Massachusetts.

Second place went to Jessica Scascitelli of Sandown, New Hampshire, who won Best Interview and tied for first place in the swimsuit competition with finalist Serena Letendre. Third place went to Darlene Leal of Dracut, Massachusetts; fourth to Jenelle Jones of North Reading, Massachusetts; and fifth to Serena Letendre of Methuen, Massachusetts. Cara Shepard of Hampton was chosen Miss Congeniality.

Organizing the pageant was Stephanie Lussier, who was still recovering from injuries sustained in a motorcycle accident. She kept the prizes as in former years: first place received $500 in cash, a trophy, sash, crown, and a photo package; the four runners-up received trophies and $300, $200, $100, and $100 respectively. The prize money was derived from the contestants' $100 application fees.

Dana Rosengard of Haverhill, Massachusetts was the pageant emcee. The judges were Valier Gosselin, Maribeth Mello, Julie Ryan, Scott Gray, Kevin Eklund, and 1993 Miss Hampton Beach Julene Britt.

Left: 1997 Miss Hampton Beach Julie Russell with 2nd place Jessica Scascitelli, July 27, 1997. Right: Julie Russell makes an appearance at the Hampton Christmas Parade, December 1997.

1998

SHANA JONES, WARWICK RI

1998 Miss Hampton Beach Shana Jones.

On July 26, 1998, a crowd of nearly 600 people gathered at the Seashell Stage to watch eighteen young women vie for the title of Miss Hampton Beach. From that field, judges chose as winner 17-year-old Shana Jones of Warwick, Rhode Island. She also won Best Interview, and, wearing an "electric" red suit she called a "hot tamale," finished in a three-way tie with Maren Fragala and Jessica Scascitelli in the swimsuit competition. In 1997 Shana won first runner up in the Miss Teen Rhode Island pageant, and was set to compete in the 1998 Miss Teen All-American nationals in Miami.

Second place in the overall competition went to Darlene Leal, 24, of Dracut, Massachusetts; third to Jessica Gregory, 19, of Kingston, Massachusetts; fourth to Rachel Arruda, 21, of Manchester, New Hampshire; and fifth place went to Jessica Scascitelli, 19, of Sandown, New Hampshire. Cara Shepard of Hampton was again named Miss Congeniality. Jones was unable to fulfill the duties of queen and Darlene Leal went on to reign as Miss Hampton Beach.

The pageant was produced by Elizabeth Lussier and hosted by Rick Lee. Heidi Sullivan of Dance Vision Network was the choreographer. The judges were Brenda McMillan Mercier, Vogue Modeling Agency; Mike Vagnoni, Mike's Cottages in Hampton; Kristen Lamoureau, model; Kathy Ormsby, Foxwoods Casino; and Mike Koller, Exuberant Enterprises.

SHANNA CLARKE, PLAISTOW NH

1999 Miss Hampton Beach Shanna Clarke.

At the pageant held on July 25, 1999, eight young women competed for the title of Miss Hampton Beach. From that field, judges chose as winner "svelte, blond-haired" Shanna Clarke of Plaistow, New Hampshire, who also won Best Interview. She was awarded a trophy and $500, and like all beach queens, was expected to represent the beach at several Hampton events during her reigning year.

Shanna appeared in her first beauty pageant at the age of eight, in a Junior Miss Concord (New Hampshire) contest. A seasoned campaigner, she had won Miss Stratham Fair, Miss Kingston, and Miss Goffstown before winning Miss Hampton Beach. Her platform was a program called REACH 2000 to put computers in public schools. She earned a degree in business administration from Northern Essex Community College and planned to open a health and fitness club. She enjoyed pageantry's competitive aspects, she said, because they reminded her of life's important lessons, like never giving up.

Second place and Miss Congeniality went to Amanda Dumont of Tyngsboro, Massachusetts; third place to Darlene Leal of Dracut, Massachusetts; fourth to Janelle Nicolo of Barrington, New Hampshire; and fifth to Laura Hidish of Methuen, Massachusetts. Rick Lee was the pageant emcee. Outgoing queen Darlene Leal was on hand to crown her successor.

1999

2000

2000—MEREDITH BARNETT, MANCHESTER NH

With a goal of qualifying for the Miss New Hampshire Scholarship pageant, in early July 2000 seventeen-year-old high school senior Meredith Barnett of Manchester, New Hampshire competed but did not place in the Miss Winnipesaukee (New Hampshire) pageant. One month later, on July 30, under a drizzle of wind-driven rain and the watchful eyes of 700 spectators at the Seashell Stage, she swept the field of 12 contestants to win the Miss Hampton Beach crown. This was her rookie season and only her second pageant.

Pageant emcee Rick Lee posed a question to each contestant. "What is the most exciting thing about Hampton Beach you would tell a first time visitor to the Seacoast?" he asked. Meredith, "whose natural, self-assured stage presence captivated the judges," responded by saying that the beach is a well-known resort and there is always something to do there.

Best Interview and second place in the overall competition went to 16-year-old Kristen Barry of Salem, New Hampshire. She shared the win in the swimsuit competition with 21-year-old Boston University student Amanda Dumont, who placed third. Fourth place went to 19-year-old Notre Dame College student Rochelle Dupont, and fifth to Kelly Thompson, 23, of Manchester, New Hampshire. Amy Laliberte was named Miss Congeniality. Also competing were local girls Tami Visconte of Exeter and Kristin Johannessen of Rye.

In her farewell speech, outgoing queen Shanna Clarke reflected on her battle with the cancer she had been diagnosed with in 1999. "That fight taught me to savor every single day I'm alive. It taught me to live every day of my life as if it were my last." (As of 2016, Shanna continues to speak to groups and write about her ongoing battle with the disease. Her book, *Fabulously Fighting*, was published this year.)

2001—KATIE WIDEN, RYE NH

At the pageant held on July 29, 2001, an audience of over 1,000 people gathered at the Seashell Stage to watch fifteen young women vie for the title of Miss Hampton Beach. From that field, judges chose as winner 19-year-old college student Katie Widen of Rye, New Hampshire, who also won Best Interview.

Katie, who had last competed in the pageant in 1998, told reporters that she found the opening dance number, which all contestants participated in, a bit "daunting," because she "didn't know how to dance."

Twenty-two-year-old Sarah Couture of Hampton took second place, won the swimsuit competition, and was named Miss Congeniality. Third place went to

Kristen Berry of Windham, New Hampshire; fourth to Theresa May Black of Lawrence, Massachusetts; and fifth to Serena Letendre of Methuen, Massachusetts.

Elizabeth Lussier hosted the pageant this year. Dancers from Dance Vision Network entertained and pageant director Stephanie Lussier and sister Amy sang several musical selections between competitions. Outgoing queen Meredith Barnett, unable to attend the event, sent a message to all the contestants: "Have fun, smile, and be confident."

It was reported that just after the five finalists were announced, two apparently disgruntled young women walked past the stage with a poster that read "Miss Hampton Beach should be from Hampton."

2001 Miss Hampton Beach Katie Widen is crowned by Randi Glickman, 2001 Miss Merrimack, at the Seashell Stage, July 29, 2001. In this era the winners resorted to "dipping" to make it easier for the outgoing queen to place the crown on their heads.

2002—BREANNE SILVI, NASHUA NH

At the July 28, 2002 pageant attended by an estimated 700 spectators and overseen by a cool, misty breeze, fourteen young women vied for the title of Miss Hampton Beach. From that field judges chose as winner a first-time competitor, 18-year-old Breanne Silvi of Nashua, New Hampshire, whose sponsor was Lupo's Bar & Grille on North Beach. Breanne also received the physical fitness award.

Second place went to Crystal Ann Benoit, 16, of Hampton Falls, New Hampshire; third to Elisa Gadecki of South Hadley, Massachusetts; fourth to Janelle Nicolo of Barrington, New Hampshire; and fifth place went to Lisa Lemaire of Newton, New Hampshire. Kristen Berry of Windham, New Hampshire was named Miss Congeniality.

Director Stephanie Lussier was the pageant emcee. Heidi Sullivan's Dance Vision Network dancers joined the contestants in an opening number and performed routines between judging rounds.

2003—THERESA MAY BLACK, LAWRENCE MA

At the pageant held on July 27, 2003, nineteen young women vied for the title of Miss Hampton Beach. From that field, judges chose as winner 21-year-old college student Theresa May Black of Lawrence, Massachusetts.

Kate Cendello, 23, of Danvers, Massachusetts took second place. Third place went to Tasha Barker, 18, of Dover, New Hampshire; fourth to Tami Visconte, 19, of Exeter, New Hampshire; and fifth place went to Chrissy Schultz, 20, of Putney, Vermont.

Stephanie Lussier and Elizabeth Lussier co-hosted the pageant, which featured acts by Red Star Baton Twirlers of Derry, New Hampshire and Dance Vision Network of

2003 Miss Hampton Beach Theresa May Black.

Manchester, with contestants joining the dance team in an opening number.

In her farewell speech, difficult to hear at times due to nagging winds, outgoing queen Breanne Silvi promoted beauty contests by saying that "Pageants build confidence and character in every contestant. If there's one thing you can take away from this, it is to believe in yourself."

"Have fun and be familiar with the beach. They are looking for someone who will represent the beach well."—2003 Miss Hampton Beach Theresa Black (2004).

2004

2004—MELISSA THERIAULT, MANCHESTER NH

Eighteen-year-old Melissa Theriault of Manchester, New Hampshire was a last minute entry to the Miss Hampton Beach pageant held on July 25, 2004. She entered to please her grandmother, but thought her chances of winning "were slim to none." The judges didn't see it that way, and chose her as winner from a field of 19 contestants. She later reflected that the toughest part of the pageant was wearing a bathing suit on stage in front of an audience.

Second place went to Jennifer Yarborough of Manchester, New Hampshire and third place to Janelle Pomeroy of Brighton, Massachusetts. Fourth place went to Rebecca Jane Hodges of South Hamilton, Massachusetts, who entered the pageant to honor her grandmother Sally Atkinson, Miss Hampton Beach of 1950. Fifth place and Miss Congeniality went to Christiann Unger of Danville, New Hampshire.

2002 Miss Hampton Beach Breanne Silvi hosted the pageant, which featured performances by Dance Vision Network and Red Star Baton Twirlers, and a farewell speech by outgoing queen Theresa Black who said, "I had the best time. I'll remember it always."

Finalist Rebecca Hodges, granddaughter of 1950 Miss Hampton Beach Sally Atkinson.

2005—ALEXANDRA HARRINGTON, SAUGUS MA

2005 Miss Hampton Beach Alexandra Harrington.

At the pageant held on July 31, 2005, twenty-two young women competed for the title of Miss Hampton Beach. From that field, judges chose as winner 17-year-old Alexandra Harrington of Saugus, Massachusetts, whose sponsors were the Whale's Tale Restaurant and Rosie's Ice Cream and Grill at the beach. She had competed but did not place last year, and had been a Miss Teen USA contestant. She was enrolled as an acting major at Hofstra University on Long Island, New York.

Alexandra took home a trophy and a $500 prize, and was expected to represent Hampton Beach in at least two of the four annual Hampton community events.

Second place went to Caitlin Sanders, 16, of Saugus, Massachusetts; third to Michelle DiNardo, 16, of Danvers, Massachusetts; fourth to Jessica Debonville, 19, of Groton, Massachusetts; and fifth place went to Dena Cashin of Billerica, Massachusetts.

2003 Miss Hampton Beach Theresa Black was the pageant host, with Dance Vision Network, the Manchester Wolves Arena II Football Dance Team, Ron Auger, and Heidi Sullivan Laroche performing dance routines between competitions.

In her farewell speech, outgoing queen Melissa Theriault told the audience, "There are just so many wonderful experiences" as Miss Hampton Beach.

2006

2006—ALLISON BLAIS, PITTSFIELD NH

At the pageant held on July 30, 2006, twenty-eight young women vied for the title of Miss Hampton Beach. From that field, judges selected as winner 17-year-old high school senior Allison Blais of Pittsfield, New Hampshire, the reigning Miss Rochester (New Hampshire) Fair queen. She took home a trophy, jewelry, and $500 cash. "I want to do it all," she said about representing the beach during her year as queen. "Alexandra [Harrington] is such a huge example, I just hope to be able to meet her standards."

Second place and Miss Congeniality went to Dena Cashin of Billerica, Massachusetts. Third place and Best Interview went to Erica Millet of Atkinson, New Hampshire. Fourth place went to Courtney Sanders of Saugus, Massachusetts, and fifth place went to Amanda Wright of York, Maine.

The winner of the swimsuit competition was 22-year-old Andra Soos of Bacau, Romania, who was spending the summer at Hampton Beach in her first visit to the United States. She was sponsored by Ashworth by the Sea, where she was employed as a waitress. "People from here make me feel good. Better than home," she was quoted as saying.

In February 2007 Allison pioneered the queen's bikini-clad entry into the Penguin Plunge, an event in which participants run into the frigid waters off Hampton Beach for charity. She raised $2,000 by jumping in, wearing only her "little red bikini." At the 2007 pageant she challenged her successor to take the plunge, and since then the event has been part of every queen's schedule.

2007—LEAH GRONDIN, HAMPTON NH

Seventeen-year-old high school student Leah Grondin of Hampton, who worked at a local surf shop and was part of the avid North Beach surfing scene, said she'd always dreamed of competing in Miss Hampton Beach. At the pageant held on July 29, 2007 her dreams came true (and then some) when judges chose her as winner in a field of 20 young women, making her the only queen from Hampton in the Seashell Stage era. Later that year she competed in the Miss New Hampshire Teen pageant and the East Coast Surfing Championships at Cape Hatteras, North Carolina.

Second place went to Brittany Dube of Atkinson, New Hampshire, third to Michaela Flynn, and fourth to Katie Owens of Exeter, New Hampshire, who won the swimsuit competition and shared Miss Congeniality with contestant Allison Lacroix. Fifth place went to Cyndal Todd.

Stephanie Lussier hosted the pageant, and Dance Vision Network and vocalist Victoria Whalen entertained between competition rounds. In her farewell speech, outgoing queen Allison Blais told the audience, "Miss Hampton Beach wasn't just another title, it was an honor and a privilege."

2007 Miss Hampton Beach Leah Grondin with the four finalists and outgoing queen Allison Blais (far right). Brittany Dube, 2nd left, Katie Owens, 4th left. Seashell Stage, July 29, 2007.

Leah continued the Penguin Plunge tradition set by her predecessor Allison Blais. Her quick dip in the ocean raised over $2,000 for Special Olympics. (Feb. 2008)

2007 Miss Hampton Beach Leah Grondin with artists at the Hampton Beach Sand Sculpting Contest (2008).

2008—LACY JANE FOLGER, FARMINGTON NH

At the pageant held on July 27, 2008, more than 1,000 spectators turned out to see 21 young women compete for the title of Miss Hampton Beach. From that field, judges chose as winner 19-year-old college student Lacy Jane Folger of Farmington, New Hampshire, who also won Best Interview. She was quoted as saying that the toughest part of the contest was watching her friends walk away before she did. She won Miss Boston in 2009 and Miss New Hampshire USA in 2011.

The other finalists were Kristen Brain of Methuen, Massachusetts; Brittany Dube of Atkinson, New Hampshire, who won the swimsuit competition; Kirby Nadilo of Stratham, New Hampshire; and Christy Dunn of Laconia, New Hampshire. Katie Owens of Exeter won Miss Congeniality.

Hosting the pageant was 2006 Miss Hampton Beach Allison Blais. Dance Vision Network, Stephanie Lussier, and Ronaldo Torres entertained the crowd. In her farewell speech, outgoing queen Leah Grondin told the audience, "Hampton Beach is a great place to be queen."

Outgoing queen Leah Grondin crowns 2008 Miss Hampton Beach Lacy Jane Folger at the Seashell Stage, July 27, 2008.

2009

2009—KRISTIN CROSSLAND, SEABROOK NH

At the pageant held on July 26, 2009, fifteen young women vied for the title of Miss Hampton Beach. From that field, judges chose as winner 19-year-old college student Kristin Crossland of Seabrook, New Hampshire, who said she wanted the beach to be a place for families "without stepping on cigarettes." A judge said it was her "local flavor" that set her above the rest. After her win, Kristin readily accepted the outgoing queen's challenge to take the Penguin Plunge in February, saying she had "the perfect bikini for it."

Some of Kristin's other wins were Miss Seabrook (2004), Miss Keene (2011), Miss Rockingham County (2013), and Miss Blackstone Valley (2014).

Second place went to Brittany Dube of Atkinson, New Hampshire, who won the swimsuit competition and Miss Congeniality. Third place went to Tina Nicholson of [hometown unknown], Massachusetts; fourth to Elizabeth Curette of Hampstead, New Hampshire; and fifth to Jenica Poulin of Gray, Maine.

The pageant was hosted by Leah Grondin, 2007 Miss Hampton Beach. In her farewell speech, outgoing queen Lacy Jane Folger told her successor, "Once the crown is on your head, you're truly a role model."

Little and Junior Miss Hampton Beach—On August 15, 2009, after a 12-year absence, these pageants returned to the beach to kick off the annual Children's Day Festival. Yianna Diagoslis, 9, of Townsend, Massachusetts won Little Miss for 5-to-9-year-olds. Also participating were Breanna Butland, Meaghan Shea, Ava Smith, Morgan Pierce, Lauryn St. Cyr, Amber Reardon, Kerrin Shea, McKayla Sanborn, Skylar Brown, and Mya Jones.

Sarah French, 15, of Vernon, Vermont won Junior Miss for 10-to-15-year-olds. Also participating were Kayla Charron, Emily Heino, Dominique Courchaine, and Genevieve Nelson.

2010—MEGAN COOLEY, AUBURN NH

During the onstage interview portion of the pageant held on July 25, 2010, 16-year-old Megan Cooley of Auburn, New Hampshire told the judges she saw the need to clean up the beach and promote family events. The judges liked what they saw and heard, and chose her as winner from the field of 15 young women who vied for the title of Miss Hampton Beach. In 2014 Megan won Miss New Hampshire and competed but did not place in the Miss America pageant.

Second place went to Katrina Harrington* and third to Holly Garcia of Everett, Massachusetts, a runner up in the 1996 Little Miss Hampton Beach contest. Fourth place went to Alicia Rossman,* the winner of the swimsuit competition, and fifth place went to Melissa Barra.* Amelia Rogers* was named Miss Congeniality, with Jennifer Blais Harrington* winning Best Interview. Settling into the category of pageant standard, contestants joined Dance Vision Network in an opening number. *Hometown unknown.*

In her farewell speech, outgoing queen Kristin Crossland told the audience that Miss Hampton Beach had been "the door to many opportunities I may not have had the confidence to try before."

Little and Junior Miss Hampton Beach—Fifteen entrants competed this year in the Little Miss pageant, with ten entrants competing in the Junior Miss pageant.

The winner in the Little competition was eight-year-old Lauryn St. Cyr, who

won second place in 2009. Runners up were Alexandra Rose Dumais, Breanna Butland, and Nicole Tramack.

The winner in the Junior competition was 14-year-old Sidney Scott, who won second place in 2009. Runners up were Victoria Soucy, Emily Croteau, and Alyssa Demelle.

"I tell the judges, just give me someone to promote this beach."—Stephanie Lussier, pageant organizer and 1995-96 Miss Hampton Beach (2010).

2011

2011—KAYLA LAYTON, BEDFORD NH

Due to ongoing construction of the Seashell Pavilion that replaced the old Seashell Stage, this year's pageant was held on a temporary stage that had been set up north of the old stage on the sands in front of the Playland Arcade.

At the pageant held on July 31, 2011, twenty-five young woman competed for the title of Miss Hampton Beach. From that field, judges chose as winner 17-year-old high school senior Kayla Layton of Bedford, New Hampshire, whose first pageant experience had been in the 2009 Miss New Hampshire Teen pageant. Kayla said that her victory at the beach, which included awards for Miss Congeniality and Best Interview, was for her grandmother Madeline Geraghty, who had been unable to attend the pageant.

Second place went to Rebecca Scalera, 21, of Derry, New Hampshire; third place and the swimsuit competition to Ashley England, 17, of Londonderry, New Hampshire; fourth to Lauren Small, 20, of Seabrook, New Hampshire; and fifth place went to 21-year-old Brittany Dube. In her farewell speech, outgoing queen Megan Cooley told the audience that being Miss Hampton Beach had given her a "huge leg up in life."

Little and Junior Miss Hampton Beach—With a combined total of 42 entrants, the pageants were busy with contestants this year. In the Little Miss pageant judges chose nine-year-old Alyson Croteau of Merrimac, Massachusetts, with runners up Sydney Cooke, Breanne Butland, Victoria D'olimpio, and Maeve Hess. In the Junior Miss pageant judges chose 13-year-old Victoria Soucy of Merrimac, Massachusetts, with runners up Alyssa Demelle, Emily Croteau, and Lilli Morales.

Left: 2011 Miss Hampton Beach judges James Malone, Scott Drohan, unknown, 2007 Miss Hampton Beach Leah Grondin, 2011 Mrs. New Hampshire Kassie Dubois, July 31, 2011.

Below left: Outgoing queen Megan Cooley crowns Kayla Layton. Below right: Kayla Layton and 2011 Jr. Miss Victoria Soucy, July 31, 2011.

2011 Miss Hampton Beach Kayla Layton with the four runners up (l-r) Brittany Dube, Rebecca Scalera, Ashley England, and Lauren Small. July 31, 2011.

2011 Little and Junior Miss Hampton Beach winners Alyson Croteau and Victoria Soucy (July 30, 2011) with (below) pageant organizer Stephanie Lussier (2012).

2012

2012—CHRISTINA DEL ROSSO, HAVERHILL MA

At the pageant held at the new Seashell Pavilion on an unseasonably cold and windy July 29, 2012, nineteen young women vied for the title of Miss Hampton Beach. From that field, judges chose as winner 16-year-old high school student Christina Del Rosso of Haverhill, Massachusetts. A childhood cancer survivor, she was involved with Relay for Life, a fundraiser for the American Cancer Society. She was a lifeguard, a cheerleader, and in 2010 won Miss Massachusetts Junior Teen. Her career goal was to work at E! Entertainment Television.

Second place went to Rebecca Scalera of Manchester, New Hampshire; a third place split went to Brittany Dube and Alexandra Barros of Medway, Massachusetts;

fifth place and the swimsuit competition went to Aria Rich of Dracut, Massachusetts. Barros won Best Interview and Lauren Small of Seabrook, New Hampshire was named Miss Congeniality. The pageant was hosted by 2010 Miss Hampton Beach Megan Cooley.

Little and Junior Miss Hampton Beach—In the Little and Junior Miss pageants, judges chose as winners nine-year-old Maeve Hess of Bradford, Massachusetts and 13-year-old Emily Croteau of Merrimac, Massachusetts.

Above: 2012 Miss Hampton Beach Christina Del Rosso, 2012 Junior Miss Emily Croteau, and 2012 Little Miss Maeve Hess attend the Hampton Beach Children's Festival (August 2012).

Right: 2012 Little Miss Maeve Hess and 2012 Junior Miss Emily Croteau attend the Hampton Beach Easter Egg Dig (March 30, 2013).

2013—GINA BRAZAO, SCITUATE MA

At the pageant held on July 28, 2013 (another unseasonably cold and windy day), ten young women competed for the title of Miss Hampton Beach. From that field, judges chose as winner 17-year-old high school senior Gina Brazao of Scituate, Massachusetts. She was a member of her high school student council and planned to study broadcast journalism in college. Gina went on to win Miss Middlesex County (2015), Miss Mayflower (2016), and was a semi-finalist in the Miss Massachusetts Scholarship pageant (2016).

Second place went to 20-year-old Brooke Riley of Lowell, Massachusetts (the 2016 winner). Third place and Miss Congeniality went to Etta Popek, 16, of Wilton, Massachusetts; fourth place and the swimsuit win went to Taylor Kudalis, 18, of

Pelham, New Hampshire; and fifth place went to Alexandra Barros, 19, of Medway, Massachusetts (the 2014 winner).

Hosting this year's pageant was 2008 Miss Hampton Beach Lacy Jane Folger. Dance Vision Network performed between competition rounds, and pageant organizer Stephanie Lussier and sister Amy sang a duet during the show. In her farewell speech, outgoing queen Christina Del Rosso said her year under the beach crown was one of "learning and growth that I will never forget."

Little and Junior Miss Hampton Beach—In the 2013 Little Miss pageant judges chose Caitlyn Kouralidis from a field of 22 contestants. Second through fifth: Riley Jean Guthrie, Emma Dumont, Samantha Spivack, Rowan Hess. McKenzie Felch was named Little Miss Congeniality. In the Junior Miss pageant judges chose Sydney Cooke from a field of 15 contestants. Second through fifth: Kaley Missert, Lexi Kaitlin Taylor, Lacey Morando, Anne-Marie Alukonis. Elena Reola was named Junior Miss Congeniality.

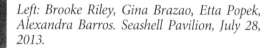

Left: Brooke Riley, Gina Brazao, Etta Popek, Alexandra Barros. Seashell Pavilion, July 28, 2013.

Below: Outgoing queen Christina Del Rosso crowns 2013 Miss Hampton Beach Gina Brazao. Seashell Pavilion, July 28, 2013.

2
0
1
4

2014—ALEXANDRA BARROS, MEDWAY MA

At the pageant held on July 27, 2014—when, for the third year in a row, the weather was less than ideal for an outdoor event—fifteen young women competed for the title of Miss Hampton Beach. This year turned out to be lucky number three for 20-year-old Alexandra Barros of Medway, Massachusetts, who had been a finalist in 2012 and 2013. A model and accomplished equestrian, she was crowned Miss Summer Nationals in 2013, was a Miss Tennessee International Junior Miss semi-finalist in 2014, and won Miss Vermont World in 2015.

Second place went to Logan Sanborn, who tied with third place Brooke Riley of Lowell, Massachusetts in the swimsuit competition. Fourth place went to Sarah Judge and fifth to Victoria Soucy of Merrimac, Massachusetts, who won Best Interview. Etta Popek of Wilton, Massachusetts was voted Miss Congeniality.

Sheila Scott, Miss Hampton Beach of 1964, returned to the beach as a judge in the pageant that she said had "opened the door" to her careers as singer, ski instructor, and beauty pageant judge. In her farewell speech, outgoing queen Gina Brazao advised her successor, "Really take in what you are about to experience, because it's over in the blink of an eye."

Little and Junior Miss Hampton Beach—In the 2014 Little Miss pageant judges chose seven-year-old Olivia Grace Scharr of Deerfield, New Hampshire from a field of 20 contestants. Second through fifth: Samantha Spivack of Natick, Massachusetts; Nianna Merrill of Auburn, New Hampshire; Keira Amirault of Goffstown, New Hampshire; Sienna Elizabeth Szarek of Pelham, New Hampshire. Halisa Carter was voted Miss Congeniality.

In the Junior Miss pageant judges chose 15-year-old Alyssa Croft of Beverly, Massachusetts from a field of 15 contestants. Second through fifth: Emma Dumont of Hampton; Lexi Taylor of Rochester, New Hampshire; Sophie Rancourt of Dover, New Hampshire; Kaylee Vance of Greenland, New Hampshire. Maeve Hess of Bradford, Massachusetts was voted Miss Congeniality.

2014 Miss Hampton Beach Ali Barros with Little Miss Olivia Scharr (left) and Junior Miss Alyssa Croft (right).

2015

2015—VICTORIA SOUCY, MERRIMAC MA

At the pageant held on July 26, 2015, a day that threatened rain but didn't deliver, nine contestants vied for the title of Miss Hampton Beach. From that field, judges chose as winner 17-year-old high school senior Victoria Soucy of Merrimac, Massachusetts, who had won Junior Miss Hampton Beach in 2011. Sponsored by her mother and the Purple Urchin Restaurant, this was Victoria's second try for the title.

The four runners up were Sarah French of Connecticut; Taylor Kudalis of Pelham, New Hampshire; Amanda Maruco of Plainville, Massachusetts; and Brooke Riley of Lowell, Massachusetts.

The host of this year's pageant was 2013 Miss Hampton Beach Gina Brazao. As pageant organizer Stephanie Lussier explained in a 2016 interview, "The year after a young woman wins she comes back to hand over her crown to the next winner. The next year I make her emcee and the fourth year she comes back as a judge."

Dancers from Heidi Sullivan Laroche's Dance Vision Network performed numbers between competitions. In her farewell speech, outgoing queen Alexandra Barros summed up nicely the impact the beach queen tradition has had on the community. "I met a little girl dressed as Miss Hampton Beach 2020," she said. "She told me she was going to wear my crown someday."

From one beach tradition to another: After her win, Victoria Soucy told a reporter, "The first thing I want to do is go to Blink's and get fried dough."

2015 Miss Hampton Beach Victoria Soucy, outgoing queen Ali Barros, the 2015 Little and Junior Misses, Rowan and Maeve Hess. Seashell Pavilion, July 26, 2015.

Little and Junior Miss Hampton Beach—In the Little Miss pageant, judges chose seven-year-old Rowan Hess of Bradford, Massachusetts from a field of 15 contestants. The runners up were all New Hampshire girls—Shay Gillis of Stratham, Lauren Brophy of North Hampton, Samantha Lemay of Deerfield, and Lexi Taylor of Rochester.

In the Junior Miss pageant, judges chose 12-year-old Maeve Hess, Rowan's sister and the 2012 Little Miss winner, from a field of 29 contestants. Second through fifth: Cecelia LeBlanc of Londonderry, New Hampshire; Cecelia's sister Olivia; Skylar Caisse of Merrimack, New Hampshire; Norah Primack of Amesbury, Massachusetts.

Pageant organizer Stephanie Lussier on stage with sisters Maeve and Rowan Hess, the 2015 Junior and Little Miss Hampton Beach winners. Seashell Pavilion, July 26, 2015.

"We're looking for the same qualities that we look for in Miss Hampton Beach. And we want a cute little kid that wants to represent Hampton Beach."
—Stephanie Lussier (2014).

2015 Miss Hampton Beach Victoria Soucy and Little Miss Rowan Hess at the 2016 Hampton Beach Easter Egg Dig (March 2016).

2016 MISS HAMPTON BEACH
BROOKE RILEY, LOWELL MA

HAMPTON HISTORICAL SOCIETY SPONSORSHIP

Brooke Riley is the first recipient of a yearly photo package donated to the pageant by the Hampton Historical Society. This sponsorship recognizes the importance of Miss Hampton Beach in the community and ensures that professional photographs of future winners are saved for posterity in the Society's collections.

List of Winners by Era and Year

CARNIVAL WEEK ERA 1915-1940   26 winners
1915 Blanche Thompson, Haverhill MA
1916 Mrs. Clara Dudley, Hampton NH
1917 Madeline Higgins, Haverhill MA
1918 Adeline Stevens, Hampton NH
1919 May Ash, Lawrence MA
1920 Lulu M. Roberts, Exeter NH
1921 Frances Fay Ford, Brighton MA
1922 Constance Block, North Hampton NH
1923 Bertha Dupleissis, Manchester NH
1924 Mildred Dudley, Hampton NH
1925 Bobbie Rowell, Hampton NH (won again in 1939)
1926 Marian Gilmore, Exeter NH
1927 Charlotte Bristol, Hampton NH
1928 Mae Fountain, Lawrence MA
1929 Doris Spackman, Portsmouth NH
1930 Dorothy Dudley, Hampton NH
1931 Edith Webster, Hampton NH
1932 Mabel Fitzgerald, Salisbury MA
1933 Phyllis Tucker, Hampton NH
1934 Blanche Hamilton, Orange MA
1935 Catherine Sargent, Hampton NH
1936 Pauline Whitehouse, Haverhill MA
1937 Delores Gauron, Hampton NH
1938 Dorothy Mitchell, Hampton NH
1939 Mrs. Bobbie Rowell Cann, Hampton NH
1940 Kathryn Sullivan, Medford MA

GALA WEEK & VICTORY WEEK 1941-1945
1941 Gala Week | Doris Bragg, Hampton NH
    Doris won the ticket-selling contest, but as there was no Carnival Queen
    named this year she is not counted in the total number of winners.
1942 Victory Week, no queen
1943 Victory Week, no queen
1944 Victory Week, no queen
1945 Victory Week, no queen

COVER GIRL YEARS 1946-1947   2 winners
1946 Marilyn Eaton, Durham NH
1947 Lois Yell, Hampton NH

AT THE BANDSTAND 1948-1958   11 winners
1948 Lorraine Doucette, Amesbury MA
1949 Caryle Cadario, Arlington MA
1950 Sally Atkinson, Ipswich MA

1951 Sonya-Bunty Romer, Montreal QB
1952 Gaynor Jenkins, Montreal QB
1953 Joan Ahearn, North Chelmsford MA
1954 Priscilla McNally, Haverhill MA
1955 Barbara Ann Curran, Waltham MA
1956 Cynthia Fuller, Brighton MA
1957 Sally Ann Freedman, Peabody MA
1958 Carolyn Komant, Kittery ME

BALLROOM ERA 1959-1976   18 winners
1959 Dianne Lipson, Cranston, RI
1960 Diane Jesak, Dracut, MA
1961 Sandie Kay, Plaistow NH
1962 Jonnye McLeod, Hampton NH
1963 Beverly Ann Hebert, Manchester NH
1964 Sheila Scott, Hampton NH
1965 Judy Reynolds, Manchester NH
1966 Marylee Houle, Worcester MA
1967 Sally Ann Gaines, Durham NH
1968 Gretchen Wood, West Newbury MA
1969 Eileen O'Connor, Lynnfield MA
1970 Janice Janes, Lynn MA
1971 Jane Floren, Bradford MA
1972 Peggy Ann Jacobson, Simsbury CT
1973 Pamela Chaffee, Epping NH
1974 Temple Bruner, Groton, MA
1975 Mara Zwemke, Greenfield MA
1976 Debra Maurice, Springfield MA

CLUB CASINO ERA 1977-1996   18 winners
1977 Tara Donnelly, North Andover, MA
1978 Kim Fontaine, Worcester MA
1979 Louise McDevitt, Lakewood CO
1980 Kathleen Rogers, Seabrook NH
1981 Diane McGarry, Manchester NH
1982 Debbie Peltonovich, Newton, NH
1983 Caron Leslie Caetano, Woburn MA
1984 Adriana Molinari, Hampton NH (orig. Uruguay)
1985 Maryanne Montagano, Dover NH
1986 Darla Beth Jelley, Manchester NH
1987 Heather Cholewa, Exeter NH
1988 Lisa Parnpichate, Thailand and West Swanzey NH
1989-90 Sabrina Dennison, Portsmouth NH
1990 Pageant canceled
1991 Maribeth Brown, Holliston MA

List of Winners by Era and Year

1992 Jennifer DiDomenico, Hampton Falls NH
1993 Julene Britt, Woburn MA
1994 Lori Greene, Boston MA
1995-96 Stephanie Lussier, Manchester NH
1996 Pageant canceled

THE SEASHELL STAGE 1997-2015   19 winners
1997 Julie Russell, Woburn MA
1998 Shana Jones, Warwick RI
1999 Shanna Clarke, Plaistow NH
2000 Meredith Barnett, Manchester NH
2001 Katie Widen, Rye NH
2002 Breanne Silvi, Nashua NH
2003 Theresa Black, Lawrence MA
2004 Melissa Theriault, Manchester NH
2005 Alexandria Harrington, Saugus MA
2006 Allison Blais, Pittsfield NH
2007 Leah Grondin, Hampton NH
2008 Lacy Jane Folger, Farmington NH
2009 Kristin Crossland, Seabrook NH
2010 Megan Cooley, Auburn NH
2011 Kayla Layton, Bedford NH
2012 Christina Del Rosso, Haverhill MA
2013 Gina Brazao, Scituate MA
2014 Alexandra Barros, Medway MA
2015 Victoria Soucy, Merrimac MA

Colorado 1
Connecticut 1
Maine 1
Massachusetts 39
New Hampshire 48
Quebec, Canada 2
Rhode Island 2
Total winners 94

Carnival Queen/Miss Hampton Beach Timeline

1915	The Hampton Beach Board of Trade is formed. Its members organize the first annual Carnival Week, at which the first Carnival Queen "popularity vote" contest is held. The first queen is crowned on an improvised stage near the bandstand.
1917	US enters WWI.
1918	Carnival Queen contestants solicit funds for the Red Cross. Armistice signed November 11, 1918.
1927	The Board of Trade becomes the Chamber of Commerce.
1929	The Chamber of Commerce erects a "Singing Tower" at their beachfront building to broadcast announcements and concerts. They later add a live amateur talent contest broadcast.
1936	The bandstand is improved with a stage and loudspeakers.
1940	The last year of the Carnival Queen.
1941-45	US fights in WWII. Carnival Week and the queen contest are put on hold. Women raise funds for charity programs and help sell war bonds instead.
1946-47	The Beachcomber Miss Cover Girl beauty pageant is held at the bandstand. Carnival Week is restarted.
1948	Miss Cover Girl is renamed Miss Hampton Beach.
1948-1958	Miss Hampton Beach is held at the beach bandstand with free admission.
1951-1967	Coronation Balls are held at the Casino Ballroom. The ball was eliminated starting with the 1968 season.
1954	Carnival Week is replaced with a month-long August Festival.
1954-1956	Weekly August beauty contests are held at the bandstand: Miss Sea Nymph, Miss Mermaid, Miss Glamour, Miss August Festival, Miss Sunshine, and Miss Personality.
1956	Inaugural Miss New Hampshire (for Miss Universe) pageant is held at Hampton Beach. Point scoring replaces the winner-by-applause system of judging. Miss Hampton Beach winners are eligible to compete in Miss Universe prep pageants; when this affiliation ended is unclear. The date of Miss Hampton Beach pageant moves from the end to the beginning of August. The crowning of the winner is combined with the coronation ball at the end of August. Contestants now required to be between the ages of 16-24 and never married.
1957-1965	Miss New England pageant is held at Hampton Beach.
1959-1995	Miss Hampton Beach is held in the Casino Ballroom with paid admission.
1962	The beach bandstand is demolished and replaced with the Seashell complex.
1966-67	Miss Hampton Beach pageants are held at the Seashell Stage.

Carnival Queen/Miss Hampton Beach Timeline

1968	Miss Hampton Beach contest and crowning are combined into a single one-night event in the Casino Ballroom.
1969	First evening gown competition. Winner is eligible to compete in the Miss USA-World pageant in Baltimore.
1976-77	Fred Shaake and others buy the Casino. They renovate the Ballroom and rename in Club Casino.
1978	An all-time ticketed audience and contestant record is set with 1,400 spectators and 61 contestants in the Club Casino.
1983	The Miss Hampton Beach pageant is videotaped and shown on the local cable channel for the first time.
1985-86	Miss Hampton Beach is a qualifying pageant for the Miss New Hampshire Scholarship, a Miss America pageant affiliate. Consequently, a talent competition is added to the pageant.
1987	Miss Hampton Beach switches affiliation to Miss New Hampshire-Miss USA pageant, eliminating the talent requirement. When this affiliation ended is unclear; the last newspaper mention was in 1991.
1989	The first deaf contestant, Sabrina Dennison, wins the title.
1990	Miss Hampton Beach is canceled. Reigning queen Sabrina Dennison represents the beach for a second year. US enters Gulf War.
1991	Pageant is dedicated to troops of Operation Desert Storm.
1996	Miss Hampton Beach is canceled again; the Chamber of Commerce ends its primary sponsorship of the pageant. Reigning queen Stephanie Lussier represents the beach for a second year. The First Annual Little and Junior Miss Hampton Beach pageants are held.
1997	Stephanie Lussier takes over management of the pageant, moving it from the Casino Ballroom to the Seashell Stage. The pageant is restarted as a free community event held outdoors on a Sunday afternoon in late July. The Little and Junior Miss pageants are suspended indefinitely.
2007	In February, 2006 Miss Hampton Beach Allison Blais is the first queen to don a bikini and take the Penguin Plunge for charity.
2009	Little and Junior Miss Hampton Beach pageants are re-introduced, held on the Saturday before the main pageant.
2011-12	The Seashell is demolished and replaced by the Seashell Pavilion. The 2011 Miss Hampton Beach pageant is held on a temporary stage nearby.
c. 2013	The Hampton Beach Village District becomes a pageant sponsor.
2016	Hampton Historical Society volunteers produce "100 Years At The Beach," a 50-minute video documenting the 100-year history of the Carnival Queens and Miss Hampton Beach beauty pageant. The Society votes to fund the current and future winners' official photograph.

Photo and Image Credits

Front cover: Jr. Miss Hampton Beach parade float, c. 1950s. Harold Fernald Collection, HHSA.

Back cover: Hampton Beach postcard, c. 1980s. HHSA.

Page 1, opposite: J. Frank Walker Hampton Beach photographs, c. 1920. HHSA.

Page 1: Board of Trade members, c. 1915. Carole Wheeler Walles, Dudley Family Collection.

Page 2: Carnival Queen Blanche Thompson and aviator J. Chauncey Redding, 1915. HHSA.

Page 4: Carnival Queen Mrs. Clara Dudley, 1916. Carole Wheeler Walles, Dudley Family Collection.

Page 6: Aviators J. Howard Bushway and Farnum Fish, 1916. HHSA.

Page 8-9: Carnival Queen Madeline Higgins, 1917. HHSA.

Page 9: 1917 Carnival Week program. HHSA.

Page 10: Adeline Stevens, 1915; Lewis F. Stevens, c. 1915; Red Cross Carnival, c. 1919. HHSA.

Page 11: Carnival Queen and King, Mae Ash and Bill Bigley, 1919; Bill Bigley, 1922; Mae Ash, 1919. HHSA.

Page 12: Carnival Week advertisement, Hampton Union, August 1921.

Page 13: Reverend Ira Jones and Vina Jones, c. 1920; Merrimack aeroplane at Hampton Beach, c. 1921. HHSA.

Page 14: Hampton Beach street scene, c. 1925. HHSA.

Page 15: Carnival Queen advert, Hampton Beach News Guide, 27Jul1923; Carnival Cottage, 1923. HHSA.

Page 16: Farr's Fried Chicken shack, 2016. Cheryl Lassiter; Farr's Fried Chicken advertisement, unknown news clip, c. 1980. HHSA.

Page 17: Miss New England article, Hampton Beach News-Guide, 18Jul1924. HHSA; Carnival Queen Mildred Dudley, 1924. Carole Wheeler Walles, Dudley Family Collection.

Page 18: Prize garage, 1925 Carnival Week program. HHSA; Bathing beauty winners, Haverhill Gazette, 11Sep1925.

Page 19: Allo Diavolo, unknown news clip; Hal McDonnell Band, c. 1925; girls on dune, 1925. HHSA.

Page 20: Carnival King and Queen William Cooper and Marion Gilmore. Manchester Union, 1926.

Page 21: Bunny and Walter White in decorated car, 1926. Carole Wheeler Walles, Dudley Family Collection; Hooker-Howe advertisement, 1925 Carnival Week program. HHSA.

Page 22: Carnival Queen Charlotte Bristol, Hampton and Hampton Beach, William Teschek (1997).

Page 23: Hughie Bancroft trade card, c. 1920. Carole Wheeler Walles, Dudley Family collection.

Page 25: Hampton Beach postcard, c, 1930. HHSA.

Page 26: Dorothy Dudley, c. 1925; Carole Wheeler, c. 1950. Carole Wheeler Walles, Dudley Family Collection.

Page 27: Hampton Beach postcard, c. 1930. HHSA.

Page 28: Phyllis Tucker photo, unknown newsclip, Judge John Perkins scrapbook. HHSA; Virginia Dennett, 1935. Robert Dennett, Dennett Family Collection.

Page 29: Phyllis Tucker as Goody Cole, 1938. HHSA; Carnival Queen Blanche Hamilton, 1934. Neume Yearbook, New England Conservatory of Music.

Page 30: Vaudeville entertainers, c. 1930; Club Cascades Review, 1935 Carnival Week Program. HHSA.

Page 31: South end Casino Ballroom, c. 1935. HHSA.

Page 32: Carnival Queen Delores Gauron, 1937. Unknown news clip, Tami Mallett; Carnival Princess Pauline DelaBarre, 1937 Vacationland magazine.

Page 33: 1938 Tercentenary billboard. HHSA; 1938 Tercentenary queens. Unknown news clip, HHSA.

Page 34: Art Deco Casino Tower (4 images), 1938. HHSA.

Page 35: 1939 Carnival Week Program. HHSA.

Page 36: 1943 Victory Week Program cover. HHSA.

Page 38: Amphibious vehicle at beach, c. 1940. HHSA.

Page 39: Bundles for Britain volunteers, 1941. HHSA.

Page 40: Casino postcard and "cafeteria" photo of beach, c. 1940s. HHSA.

Page 41: Miss Cover Girl Marilan Eaton, 1946. Original photo (published in The Beachcomber, 21Aug1946), Harold Fernald Collection, HHSA.

Page 42: 1946 Miss Cover Girl finalists, The Beachcomber, 21Aug1946. HHSA; Lillian Clarke photo and silhouettes, 1945-1967. HHSA.

Page 43: 1947 Miss Cover Girl Lois Yell. Original photo (published in The Beachcomber, 27Aug1947), Harold Fernald Collection, HHSA.

Page 44: 1947 Miss Cover Girl contestants. Original photo (published in The Beachcomber, 27Aug1947), Harold Fernald Collection, HHSA

Page 45: Bill Elliot (3 images). HHSA.

Page 46: Hampton Beach bandstand postcard, c. 1945, 1955 Miss August Festival pageant. HHSA.

Page 48: Sonja-Bunty Romer. The Beachcomber, 26Aug1953. HHSA.

Page 49: Bill Elliot, John Dineen, 1956 Miss Hampton Beach pageant. HHSA; Ted Herbert orchestra advertisement. Unknown news clip, HHSA.

Page 50: Three images. Robert Dennett, Dennett Family Collection.

Page 51: 1948 Miss Hampton Beach Lorraine Doucette, 1947 photo. From original photo (published in The Beachcomber, 27Aug1947), Harold Fernald Collection, HHSA; Miss Catalina swimsuits. The Beachcomber, 1Sep1948, HHSA.

Page 52: 1949 Miss Hampton Beach Caryl Cadario, 1947 photo. From original photo (published in The Beachcomber, 27Aug1947), Harold Fernald Collection, HHSA.

Page 53: *1950 Miss Hampton Beach Sally Atkinson (2 images). Marilyn Atkinson Tilbury, Atkinson Family Collection.*

Page 54: *1951 Miss Hampton Beach Sonja Bunty Romer, from the 1952 coronation of Gaynor Jenkins. HHSA.*

Page 55: *1952 Miss Hampton Beach Gaynor Jenkins. HHSA.*

Page 56: *1952 Miss Hampton Beach. HHSA.*

Page 57: *Carole Wheeler, c. 1950. Carole Wheeler Walles, Dudley Family Collection.*

Page 58: *1953 Miss Hampton Beach Joan Ahearn, unknown news clip and photo, HHSA.*

Page 59: *1953 Miss Hampton Beach court. HHSA.*

Page 60: *1954 Miss Hampton Beach Priscilla McNally and king. HHSA.*

Page 61: *1954 Miss Hampton Beach Priscilla McNally and king. HHSA.*

Page 62: *Barbara Ann Curran. Unknown 1956 news clip, HHSA; 1955 Miss Hampton Beach and court. Hampton Union, 8Sep1955, HHSA.*

Page 63: *Cynthia Fuller and Barbara Ann Curran, 1956, HHSA; 1956 Miss Hampton Beach winners. Hampton Union, 9Aug1956, HHSA.*

Page 64: *1956 Coronation Ball. HHSA.*

Page 65: *1956 Miss New Hampshire. Unknown news clip; 1957 Miss New England. The Beachcomber, 14Aug1957, HHSA.*

Page 66: *1994 Miss Personality (3 images). HHSA.*

Page 67: *1954 Miss Sea Nymph. Hampton Union, 2Sep1954, HHSA; 1954 Miss Sunshine. Hampton Union, 26Aug1954, HHSA; 1955 Miss August Festival. HHSA; Ray Anthony. Unknown news clip, HHSA.*

Page 68: *1955 Miss Sea Nymph. HHSA; 1956 Miss Sea Nymph. Hampton Union, 16Aug1956, HHSA; 1956 Miss Mermaid. Hampton Union, 23Aug1956, HHSA.*

Page 69: *1957 Miss Hampton Beach Sally Ann Freedman. HHSA.*

Page 70: *1957 Miss Hampton Beach pageant. HHSA; 1957 Miss Hampton Beach crowning. HHSA; 1957 Miss Hampton Beach winners. Hampton Union, 8Aug1957, HHSA.*

Page 71: *1958 Miss Hampton Beach Carolyn Ann Komant. HHSA.*

Page 72-73: *1958 Miss Hampton Beach (4 images). HHSA.*

Page 74: *1959 and 1962 Coronation Balls. HHSA.*

Page 75: *1959 Miss Hampton Beach Diane Lipson. HHSA.*

Page 76: *1959 Miss Hampton Beach pageant. HHSA.*

Page 77: *1959 Miss Hampton Beach (top 2 images). HHSA. 1959 Miss Hampton Beach (bottom 2 images). Fred Rice, Rice Family Collection.*

Page 78: *1959 Miss Hampton Beach/Miss New England (3 images). HHSA.*

Page 79: *1959 Coronation Ball. HHSA.*

Page 80: *1960 Miss Hampton Beach Diane Laurel Jesak. HHSA.*

Page 81: *1960 Miss Hampton Beach winners. HHSA; Hampton Beach postcard, c. 1960s. HHSA.*

Page 82: *1961 Miss Hampton Beach Sandie Kay. HHSA.*

Page 83-84: *1961 Miss Hampton Beach pageant (3 images). HHSA.*

Page 85: *1961 Coronation Ball. HHSA.*

Page 86: *1962 Miss New Hampshire Sandie Kay. HHSA.*

Page 87: *1962 Miss Hampton Beach Jonnye McLeod. HHSA.*

Page 88: *Jonnye McLeod (top 2 images). Winnacunnet High School Library; 1962 Miss Hampton Beach. HHSA.*

Page 89: *1962 Miss Hampton Beach (2 images). HHSA.*

Page 90: *1962 Coronation Ball. HHSA.*

Page 91: *1963 Miss Hampton Beach Beverly Ann Hebert. HHSA.*

Page 92: *1963 Miss New England winners. Frances Houlihan, Houlihan Family Collection.*

Page 93: *1964 Miss Hampton Beach Sheila Scott. HHSA.*

Page 94: *Sheila Scott (3 images). Sheila Scott, Scott Family Collection.*

Page 95: *Stan Bednarz photo and postcard (2 images). HHSA.*

Page 96: *1965 Miss Hampton Beach Judy Reynolds. HHSA.*

Page 97-98: *1965 Miss Hampton Beach (4 images). HHSA.*

Page 99: *1966 Miss Hampton Beach Marylee Houle. HHSA.*

Page 100: *1966 Miss Hampton Beach. HHSA.*

Page 101: *1967 Miss Hampton Beach Sally Gaines. HHSA.*

Page 102: *1967 Miss Hampton Beach. Hampton Union, 27Jul1967, HHSA; 1967 Miss Hampton Beach. Sheila Scott, Scott Family Collection.*

Page 103: *1968 Miss Hampton Beach Gretchen Wood. HHSA.*

Page 104: *1969 Miss Hampton Beach Eileen O'Connor. Hampton Union, 30Jul1969 (Lane Library microfilm).*

Page 105: *1970 Miss Hampton Beach Janice Janes. Springfield Sunday Republican, 26Jul1970 (genealogybank.com).*

Page 106: *1971 Miss Hampton Beach Jane Floren. Hampton Union, 28Jul1971 (Lane Library microfilm).*

Page 107: *1972 Miss Hampton Beach Peggy Ann Jacobson. HHSA.*

Page 108: *1972 Miss Hampton Beach Peggy Ann Jacobson. Hampton Union, 26Jul1972 (Lane Library microfilm).*

Page 109-110: *1973 Miss Hampton Beach Pam Chaffee (2 images). HHSA.*

Photo and Image Credits

Page 111: 1974 Miss Hampton Beach Temple Bruner. HHSA.

Page 112-113: 1974 Miss Hampton Beach pageant (4 images). Hampton Union, 24Jul1974 (Lane Library microfilm).

Page 114: 1975 Miss Hampton Beach Mara Joan Zwemke. 1976 Hampton Beach program brochure, HHSA.

Page 115: 1975 Miss Hampton Beach Mara Joan Zwemke. HHSA.

Page 116: 1975 Miss Hampton Beach Debra Maurice. HHSA.

Page 117: Club Casino advertisement, c. 1976. Hampton Beach program brochure, HHSA.

Page 118: Fred Shaake, c. 1976. Unknown news clip, HHSA.

Page 119: Hampton Beach Casino, c. 1975 (2 images). HHSA.

Page 120: 1977 Miss Hampton Beach Tara Donnelly. 1978 Hampton Beach program brochure, HHSA.

Page 121: 1977 Miss Hampton Beach Tara Donnelly. HHSA.

Page 122: 1978 Miss Hampton Beach Kim Fontaine. HHSA.

Page 123: 1978 Miss Hampton Beach pageant. HHSA.

Page 124: 1979 Miss Hampton Beach Louise McDevitt. HHSA.

Page 125: Hampton Beach program brochures. HHSA.

Page 126: 1980 Miss Hampton Beach Kathleen Ann Rogers. HHSA.

Page 128: 1981 Miss Hampton Beach Diane McGarry. HHSA.

Page 129: 1982 Miss Hampton Beach Debbie Peltonovich. HHSA.

Page 130: 1982 Miss Hampton Beach pageant (2 images). HHSA.

Page 131: Top left image, Hampton Union, 13Jul1983, HHSA; center left image, Hampton Union, 13Jul1983, HHSA; bottom left image, The Beachcomber, 21Jul1983, HHSA; right image, HHSA.

Page 132: 1983 Miss Hampton Beach Caron Leslie Caetano. HHSA.

Page 133: The Continentals. Unknown news clip, HHSA; 1983 Hampton Beach program brochure, HHSA.

Page 134: 1983 Miss Hampton Beach pageant (4 images). Chamber of Commerce scrapbook, HHSA.

Page 135: 1983 Miss Hampton Beach (bottom image). Hampton Union, 27Jul1983 (Lane Library microfilm); 1983 Miss Hampton Beach (top image). Chamber of Commerce scrapbook, HHSA.

Page 136: 1984 Miss Hampton Beach Adriana Molinari. HHSA.

Page 137: 1984 Miss Hampton Beach winners. Atlantic News, 2Aug1984, Chamber of Commerce scrapbook, HHSA.

Page 138: 1985 Miss Hampton Beach Maryanne Molinari. HHSA.

Page 139: 1985 Hampton Beach program brochure. HHSA.

Page 140: 1986 Miss Hampton Beach Darla Beth Jelley. HHSA.

Page 141: 1986 Miss Hampton Beach pageant (2 images). Hampton Union, 16Jul1986 (Lane Library microfilm).

Page 142: 1987 Miss Hampton Beach Heather Cholewa. HHSA.

Page 143: 1987 Hampton Beach program brochure, HHSA; 1987 Miss Hampton Beach (2 images). HHSA.

Page 144: 1988 Miss Hampton Beach Lisa Parnpichate. HHSA.

Page 145: 1988 Miss Hampton pageant, winner in beach parade (3 images). HHSA.

Page 146: 1989-90 Miss Hampton Beach Sabrina Dennison. HHSA.

Page 147: 1989 Hampton Beach program brochure. HHSA; 1989-90 Miss Hampton Beach Sabrina Dennison on horseback. HHSA; newspaper headline (center left). Hampton Union, 10Jul1990 (Lane Library microfilm).

Page 148: 1991 Miss Hampton Beach Maribeth Brown. HHSA.

Page 149: 1991 Miss Hampton Beach with Glen French, 1991 Miss Hampton Beach contestants. HHSA.

Page 150: 1992 Miss Hampton Beach Jennifer DiDomenico. HHSA.

Page 151: 1992 Miss Hampton Beach contestants, pageant, Hampton Beach program brochure. HHSA.

Page 152: 1993 Miss Hampton Beach Julene Britt. HHSA.

Page 153: 1993 Miss Hampton Beach pageant (2 images), Hampton Beach program brochure. HHSA.

Page 154: 1993 Miss Hampton Beach pageant (2 images). HHSA.

Page 155: 1994 Miss Hampton Beach Lori Green. HHSA.

Page 156: 1994 Miss Hampton Beach Lori Green, Hampton Beach program brochure, pageant tickets. HHSA.

Page 157: 1995 Miss Hampton Beach Stephanie Lussier. HHSA.

Page 158: 1995 Miss Hampton Beach 50th anniversary program. HHSA.

Page 159: 1995 Miss Hampton Beach pageant (3 image). HHSA.

Page 160: Composite photograph of the old and new Seashells. Composite by Cheryl Lassiter from HHSA photos.

Photo and Image Credits

Page 162-163: 1997 Miss Hampton Beach Julie Russell (3 images). HHSA.

Page 164: 1998 Miss Hampton Beach Shana Jones. Unknown news clip courtesy of Shanna Clarke.

Page 165: 1999 Miss Hampton Beach Shanna Clarke. Unknown news clip courtesy of Shanna Clarke.

Page 166: 2000 Miss Hampton Beach Meredith Barnett. Courtesy of Stephanie Lussier.

Page 168: 2001 Miss Hampton Beach Katie Widen. Courtesy of Katie Widen Reardon.

Page 169: 2001 Miss Hampton Beach pageant. Courtesy of Katie Widen Reardon.

Page 170: 2002 Miss Hampton Beach Breanne Silvi. Hampton Union, 30Jul2002 (Lane Library microfilm).

Page 171: 2003 Miss Hampton Beach Theresa Black. Hampton Union, 29Jul2003 (Lane Library microfilm).

Page 172: 2004 Miss Hampton Beach Melissa Theriault. Hampton Union, unknown issue; contestant Rebecca Hodges. Marilyn Tilbury, Atkinson Family Collection.

Page 173: 2005 Miss Hampton Beach Alexandra Harrington. HHSA.

Page 174-175: 2006 Miss Hampton Beach Allison Blais. Courtesy of John Kane, Hampton Beach Village District.

Page 176: 2007 Miss Hampton Beach Leah Grondin. HHSA.

Page 177: 2007 Miss Hampton Beach, top and bottom right images courtesy of John Kane, Hampton Beach Village District; Bottom left photo. HHSA.

Page 178: 2008 Miss Hampton Beach Lacy Jane Folger. Courtesy of John Kane, Hampton Beach Village District.

Page 179: 2008 Miss Hampton Beach pageant. Top and bottom photos courtesy of Stephanie Lussier, center photo courtesy of John Kane, Hampton Beach Village District.

Page 180: 2009 Miss Hampton Beach Kristin Crossland (2 images). Courtesy of John Kane, Hampton Beach Village District.

Page 181: 2010 Miss Hampton Beach Megan Cooley (2 images). Courtesy of John Kane, Hampton Beach Village District.

Page 182: Pageant director Stephanie Lussier in 2016. Courtesy of Cheryl Lassiter.

Page 183: 2011 Miss Hampton Beach Kayla Layton. Courtesy of John Kane, Hampton Beach Village District.

Page 184: 2011 Miss Hampton Beach pageant. Top and bottom left photos courtesy of Stephanie Lussier; bottom right photo courtesy of John Kane, Hampton Beach Village District.

Page 185: 2011 Miss Hampton Beach pageant winners, top photo courtesy of Stephanie Lussier; bottom photos courtesy of John Kane, Hampton Beach Village District.

Page 186: 2012 Miss Hampton Beach Christina Del Rosso. Courtesy of John Kane, Hampton Beach Village District.

Page 187: 2012 contests winners (2 images). Courtesy of John Kane, Hampton Beach Village District.

Page 188: 2013 Miss Hampton Beach Gina Brazao. Hampton Union, 25Jul2014 (Lane Library microfilm).

Page 189: 2013 winners (2 images). Courtesy of Stephanie Lussier.

Page 190: 2014 Miss Hampton Beach Alexandra Barros. HHSA.

Page 191: 2014 winners. Courtesy of John Kane, Hampton Beach Village District.

Page 192-193: 2015 Miss Hampton Beach Victoria Soucy (2 images). Courtesy of Stephanie Lussier.

Page 194: 2015 Little, Junior, and Miss winners (2 images). Courtesy of John Kane, Hampton Beach Village District.

Page 195: 2016 Miss Hampton Beach Brooke Riley, HHSA

Notes

(Page) 1. "parade of bathing girls." *Hamptons Union, 06Sep1917;* "popularity votes." *Hamptons Union, 02Aug1917.*

3. "with a little help from her Dad." *The Beachcomber, 08Jul1971;* "the most thrilling ever seen," "the art of aerial warfare." *Hamptons Union, 09Sep1915.*

4. "the full freedom…" *Hamptons Union, 07Sep1916;* "expressed her experience…" *Hamptons Union, 14Sep1916;* "diamond rings of value." *Hamptons Union, 24Aug1916.*

5. "nine months actual experience…" *Hamptons Union, 14Sept1916;* "If you couldn't learn to fly…" *Santa Cruz Sentinel, 14Jul1971.*

6. "Hair-raising stunts…," "rattle trap." *Oakland Tribune, 25Dec1927.*

7. "nine motorcyclists…" *Portsmouth Herald, 10Jul1916;* "Latest in Aviation," "one of the most successful," "near I Street," "finely executed," "long trip to the southerly part," *Hamptons Union, 14Sep1916;* "demonstrations of aerial bombardment…" *Hamptons Union, 17Aug1916;* "easily," *Hamptons Union, 07Sep1916.*

8. "in all his regal robes…," "aerial bombs and the cheers," "rule supreme," *Hamptons Union, 16Aug1917;* "gaily decorated," "parade of bathing girls," *Hamptons Union, 06Sep1917.*

11. "Victory Avenues of the Allies," *Hamptons Union, 28Aug1919.*

12. "7 Aladdin-like days and nights," *Portsmouth Herald, 3Sep1921;* "The Pageant of Hampton," "historical and allegorical," *Hamptons Union 04Aug1921.*

13. "drop inflated tubes," *Hamptons Union, 01Sep1921.*

14. "Princeton's famous all-around athlete," *Hampton Beach News-Guide, 22Jul1922;* "Spirit of Hampton," *Hamptons Union, 31Aug1922.*

15. "Portable house," *Hampton Beach News-Guide, 27Jul1923.*

16. "Do You Know," *Hampton Beach News-Guide, 13Jul1923.*

17. "witnessed by fully 30,000 persons," *Boston Daily Globe, 07Sept1924;* "pick the most beautiful bathing girl," "a chaperone of her own choosing," *Hampton Beach News-Guide, 04Jul1924;* "Neptune's Daughter…" *Hampton Beach News-Guide, 04Aug1924.*

18. "Coronation Mardi Gras Parade," *1925 Carnival Week Program;* "rube cop," *Haverhill Gazette, 11Sep1925.*

20. "By the hand of…," "winter," "prettiest," *Manchester Union, 10Sep1926.*

22. "identified as Charlotte Bristol," see *Hampton and Hampton Beach by William Teschek, p. 126;* "in addition to…," "the queen and her…," "crown princess," *Hamptons Union, 30Jun1927.*

23. "royal consort," *Hamptons Union, 13Sep1928.*

24. "King Karnival…," "attendants," *Haverhill Gazette, 06Sep1929;* "$6000 Out-of-Door Concert Electrola," *Hamptons Union, 22Aug1929;* "singing tower," *Hampton Union & Rockingham County Gazette, 01Sep1932;* "realistic and amusing sketch…fire department succeeds," *Hamptons Union, 05Sep1929.*

26. "circus flying," "whose appearance with…," *Portsmouth Herald, 26Aug1930.*

27. "Hindoo pageant…master of slaves," "very beautiful in sparkling white," *Hampton Union & Rockingham County Gazette* [hereafter HURCG], *17Sep1931.*

28. "singing tower," *HURCG, 01Sep1932;* "English Bishop," "Despite cold weather..," *HURCG, 15Sep1932;* "On one of the most beautiful nights…," *HURCG, 14Sep1933.*

31. "ladies in waiting," "gentlemen of the court," *Nashua Telegraph, 07Sep1935.*

32. "With colorful pageantry…," "tiny," "Midnight in Paris," *Portsmouth Herald, 11Sep1937.*

33. "suitable," *Portsmouth Herald, 10Sep1938.*

35. "war bond booth," *Portsmouth Herald, 14Aug1945.*

37. "failed to retard business," "blue cellophane," "battle of music," *Portsmouth Herald, 10Sep1942.*

38. "snake dances…," *Portsmouth Herald, 15Aug1945;* "At 7 o'clock on Tuesday evening…," *Hampton Union, 16Aug1945.*

41. "Future Development," "mystery," *The Beachcomber, 21Aug1946.*

47. "radio star and disc jockey," *Daily Boston Globe, 28Jul1957.*

48. "vital statistics," *see for example, The Beachcomber & Rockingham County Gazette, 22Jul1964* and *Hampton Union, 19Jul1979.*

Notes

51. "Catalina Miss America," "representative of the 20th Century Fox studios…," *The Beachcomber,* *18Aug1948.*

53. "beautiful, blue-eyed and blond," "lime one-piece suit," *The Beachcomber, 23Aug1950;*

54. "tall, shapely brunette," "38-25-37," *Hampton Union, 30Aug1951.*

55. "vociferously," "over a local blond favorite…," "for not being as popular…," "sweetly slender," "panel of harried newspapermen," *Portsmouth Herald, 22Aug1952.*

60. "full slate," "clearly the spectators' favorite," *Hampton Union, 9Sep1954.*

63. "to let the queen reign…," *Hampton Union 9Aug1956.*

64. "A beauty contest which has not been attempted before…," "cool and handsome," *Daily Boston Globe, 28Jul1957.*

71. "35-23-35," *Hampton Union & Rockingham County Gazette, 31Jul1958.*

75. John Dineen remarks, *Hampton Union, 16Jul1959.*

76. "glistening silver bathing suit…," "36-23-36," "giant-size," *Hampton Union, 30Jul1959.*

91. "well-distributed pounds," "36-25-36," *The Beachcomber, 24Jul1963.*

92. "Displaying near perfect poise," *Hampton Union, 15Aug1963.*

96. Judy's "vital statistics," *The Beachcomber, 21Jul1965.*

99. "There was so much group spirit," *Hampton Union, 11Aug1966.*

101. "petite and attractive," "unanimously voted," *Hampton Union, 27Jul1967.*

104. "Would you like a seat…," "before a crowd of hundreds," *Hampton Union, 30Jul1969.*

106. "on a whim," "I've been coming to Hampton Beach…," *Hampton Union, 28Jul1971.*

108. "The most fascinating on the east coast," "aura of excitement…," *Hampton Union, 19Jul1972;* "stately beauty," "opportunity for paid radio…," *Hampton Union, 26Jul1972.*

111. "Five foot four-and-a-half-inch…," "opportunity to represent," *Hampton Union, 24Jul1974.*

114. "Such competitions in which women…," *Hampton Union, 16Jul1975.*

115. "record-breaking crowd," "5 feet, 9 inches tall…," *Hampton Union, 23Jul1975.*

116. "spending money for the trip," *The Morning Union (Springfield, Mass.), 22Jul1976.*

120. "largest crowd ever," *Hampton Union, 20Jul1977.*

121. "What do you look for…," "be very friendly…," *Hampton Union, 20Jul1977.*

123. "What do you feel is…," "America's a great country, but…," *Hampton Union 19Jul1978.*

124. "35-25-33," *Hampton Union, 18Jul1979.*

126. "pal Rusty," *Hampton Union, 16Jul1980.*

127. "not to fall off my shoes," *Hampton Union, 30Jul1980.*

129. "an articulate, vivacious blond…," "They are great entertainment…,"*Hampton Union, 21Jul1982.*

132. "a night of glitter and pageantry…," *The Beachcomber, 12Jul1983;* "a relic in pageantry," *Hampton Union, 20Jul1983.*

136. "charming South American accent," "won over the judges," *Hampton Union, 25Jul1984.*

137. "So are pageants…," *The Spokesman Review (Spokane WA), 25Feb1993.*

139. "Kaleidoscope of multi-colored…," "a great sense of humor," *Hampton Union, 21Aug1985.*

143. "a variety of tunes," *Hampton Union, 18Jul1987.*

144. "to an explosion of applause…," *Hampton Union, 26Jul1988.*

146. "5'3" and 115 lbs," *Hampton Union, 25Jul1989.*

152. "who is the most influential person…," "My Irish Catholic grandmother…," *Hampton Union, 30Jul1993.*

155. "in front of hundreds of admirers," "clear crowd favorite," *Hampton Union, 26Jul1994.*

160. "These girls are not just beauty queens…," *Hampton Union 29Jul2005.*

164. "electric," "hot tamale," *Hampton Union, 28Jul1998.*

165. "svelte, blond-haired…" *Atlantic News, 29Jul1999;* "enjoyed pageantry's competitive…," *Hampton Union, 30Jul1999.*

167. "What is the most exciting…," "whose natural self-assured stage presence…," "That fight taught me…," *Hampton Union, 1Aug2000.*

168. "daunting," "didn't know how to dance," *Hampton Union, 31Jul2001.*

169. "Have fun, smile, and be confident," "Miss Hampton Beach should be from Hampton," *Hampton Union, 31Jul2001.*
171. "Pageants build confidence...," *Hampton Union, 29Jul2003;* "Have fun and be familiar...," *Hampton Union, 23Jul2004.*
172. "thought her chances were...," "toughest part," "I had the best time...," *Hampton Union, 27Jul2004.*
173. "There are just so many...," *Hampton Union, 2Aug2005.*
174. "I want to do it all...," *Hampton Union, 1Aug2006.*
175. "People from here make me feel good...,"*Hampton Union, 1Aug2006;* "little red bikini," *Hampton Union, 31Jul2007.*
176. "An honor and a privilege...," *Hampton Union, 31Jul2007.*
178. "was watching her friends...," "...great place to be queen," *Hampton Union, 29Jul2008.*
180. "without stepping on...," "local flavor," "the perfect bikini...," *Hampton Union, 28Jul2009;* "Once the crown is on your head...," *Foster's Daily Democrat, 27Jul2009.*
182. "the door to many opportunities...," "I tell the judges...," *Hampton Union, 27Jul2010.*
184. "huge leg up in life," *Hampton Union, 2Aug2011.*
189. "learning and growth...," *Hampton Union, 23Jul2013.*
191. "opened the door," *Hampton Union, 25Jul2014;* "Really take in...," *Hampton Union, 29Jul2014.*
193. "The year after...," *Hampton Union, 1Aug2016;* "I met a little girl..." "The first thing I want to do...," *Hampton Beachcomber, 31Jul2015.*
194. "We're looking for the same qualities...," *Hampton Union, 29Jul2014.*

Index

Index

Index

Index

Index

Index

Index